teach
yourself

political philosophy

Jan Klug

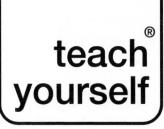

political philosophy
mel thompson

Launched in 1938, the **teach yourself** series
grew rapidly in response to the world's wartime
needs. Loved and trusted by over 50 million
readers, the series has continued to respond to
society's changing interests and passions and
now, 70 years on, includes over 500 titles,
from Arabic and Beekeeping to Yoga and Zulu.
What would you like to learn?

be where you want to be with **teach yourself**

For UK order enquiries: please contact Bookpoint Ltd, 130 Milton Park, Abingdon, Oxon OX14 4SB. Telephone: +44 (0) 1235 827720. Fax: +44 (0) 1235 400454. Lines are open 09.00–17.00, Monday to Saturday, with a 24-hour message answering service. Details about our titles and how to order are available at www.teachyourself.co.uk

For USA order enquiries: please contact McGraw-Hill Customer Services, PO Box 545, Blacklick, OH 43004-0545, USA. Telephone: 1-800-722-4726. Fax: 1-614-755-5645.

For Canada order enquiries: please contact McGraw-Hill Ryerson Ltd, 300 Water St, Whitby, Ontario L1N 9B6, Canada. Telephone: 905 430 5000. Fax: 905 430 5020.

Long renowned as the authoritative source for self-guided learning – with more than 50 million copies sold worldwide – the **teach yourself** series includes over 500 titles in the fields of languages, crafts, hobbies, business, computing and education.

British Library Cataloguing in Publication Data: a catalogue record for this title is available from the British Library.

Library of Congress Catalog Card Number: on file.

First published in UK 2008 by Hodder Education, part of Hachette Livre UK, 338 Euston Road, London, NW1 3BH.

First published in US 2008 by The McGraw-Hill Companies, Inc.

This edition published 2008.

The **teach yourself** name is a registered trademark of Hodder Headline.

Copyright © 2008 Mel Thompson

Typeset by Transet Limited, Coventry, England.
Printed in Great Britain for Hodder Education, an Hachette Livre UK Company, 338 Euston Road, London NW1 3BH, by CPI Cox & Wyman, Reading, Berkshire RG1 8EX.

The publisher has used its best endeavours to ensure that the URLs for external websites referred to in this book are correct and active at the time of going to press. However, the publisher and the author have no responsibility for the websites and can make no guarantee that a site will remain live or that the content will remain relevant, decent or appropriate.

Hachette Livre UK's policy is to use papers that are natural, renewable and recyclable products and made from wood grown in sustainable forests. The logging and manufacturing processes are expected to conform to the environmental regulations of the country of origin.

Impression number   10 9 8 7 6 5 4 3 2 1
Year   2012 2011 2010 2009 2008

contents

01

introduction

In this chapter you will learn:
- about the questions addressed by political philosophy
- why political philosophy is about values rather than descriptions
- how political ideas have developed historically
- what issues are covered by political philosophy.

What is political philosophy?

- How does politics contribute to the well-being or otherwise of humankind?
- What is the good life, and how is it achieved?
- What principles and values should be used to shape and judge political institutions?
- What sort of society will best allow its citizens to flourish?
- What do we really mean by equality, justice, freedom and so on?
- Is it ever right to go to war, or to rebel against a government?
- What responsibility should governments have for the global issues of terrorism or the environment?

Political philosophy is concerned with all these questions and many more. It is about good government – what it involves, how it is regulated and how it is brought about. It is about the principles that help us to decide whether or not any particular government is to be judged good or bad. And, of course, that requires an examination of the fundamental principles of government – why we need it, what its goals should be, how it is to be regulated and how, if it goes wrong, it may be repaired or replaced.

Political philosophy may be seen as a branch of ethics, or moral philosophy. Ethics looks at all issues of right and wrong in the way people treat one another, while political philosophy limits itself to the specific issues related to our collective or political life. It is the ethics of social organization, applied across society, rather than between individuals. So, for example, utilitarianism as an ethical theory (seeking that which appears to offer the greatest benefit for the greatest number) when applied to society as a whole, is used to justify democracy, which aims to take the preferences of all citizens into account through the democratic process.

Part of the task of political philosophy is to establish whether or not there are objective criteria for deciding between right and wrong. Does everything depend upon the wishes of the people, or are there universally rational principles for organizing good governance?

But just as ethics requires us to give a rational justification for our actions, so too political philosophy examines the justification for political institutions and ideologies. Is democracy fair to everyone? Is there such a thing as a good dictatorship? It also examines key ideas – fairness, justice, the rights of individuals or communities – to see how they are related to one another, and how what they describe may be achieved.

Would it be fair if everyone in society received an equal share of goods and services, no matter what they contributed by way of work? Or would it be fairer if everyone were allowed to earn and keep as much as they could? Should important decisions be taken by everyone, or only by those whose experience and knowledge best qualifies them to decide? These are fundamental questions – not about how society *actually* operates, but about how it *should* operate.

In other words

The shorthand way of expressing this is to say that political philosophy is **normative**. Just as ethics may be *descriptive* (this is what people do) or *normative* (this is what they should do), so politics, sociology and economics are descriptive (this is how the political system, society or the economy works) whereas political philosophy is normative (this is what constitutes a just, fair or free society).

It is equally important to appreciate what political philosophy is not. It is *not* concerned with describing actual political societies or institutions: that is the study of politics. Nor is it the study of the way in which nations and empires have developed and spread globally: that is the study of political geography (although a knowledge of politics and political geography is useful for anyone interested in political philosophy). Nor is it the study of how finance, trade and the markets shape society: that is economics. Rather, *political philosophy is concerned with the rational and normative justification of political entities.*

Political entities?

Well, yes – because 'the political' is not simply limited to what happens at a national level. International bodies are equally relevant, as may be local groups, city states, trade unions, international companies, trading systems, shareholders and directors of companies, and even families. Although contentious, you can argue that 'political' can apply to all those situations where groups of people organize themselves for mutual support or action.

Politics itself can be a practical, mechanical business – sorting out how best to deliver agreed benefits and so on. However, if it were only that, there would be few political issues to discuss – every form of government would be judged simply on the basis of its efficient delivery. But life is not that straightforward. People disagree about the principles upon which society should be run – and it is these disagreements about principles that form the basis of political philosophy.

Ends and means

'Where ends are agreed, the only questions left are those of means, and these are not political but technical ...'

'... political theory is a branch of moral philosophy, which starts from the discovery, or application, of moral notions in the sphere of political relations.'

Isaiah Berlin 'Two concepts of Liberty'
a lecture given in Oxford, 1958

In other words, political philosophy should be about ends – about what you seek to achieve through politics. Once the ends are agreed on, politics and economics are the disciplines that see to their delivery. But, of course, political and economic systems tend to generate their own ends, so these too are scrutinized within political philosophy.

Political philosophy is certainly not limited to the Western tradition. In China, for example, both Confucius and Lao Tzu wrote about how people might live together – indeed the Confucian tradition had a huge impact on Chinese culture and politics for millennia. Unfortunately, there is no room in this book to explore the history of political ideas other than those in the West, but that would be an interesting follow-up to the ideas discussed here.

Philosophy is never written in a vacuum. It is always coloured by the general assumptions and ideas of its day, even though the best philosophers ask radical questions and challenge those assumptions. Thus, for example, when we look at the work of Plato or Aristotle, we know that they are writing against the background of the politics of their day. When they talk about democracy, for example, they are not referring to modern representational democracy, but about the direct system of government where a relatively small and privileged number of people made decisions about how the city-state (or *'polis'*) should be governed. Perhaps more than in any other branch of philosophy, political philosophy therefore benefits from being seen in context. So we will start with a brief historical sketch ...

An historical perspective

Ancient Greece and the mediaeval world

As exemplified by Plato and Aristotle, the political philosophy of Ancient Greece addressed the issue of the 'good life' and how it might be lived in society. Against a range of political structures of their day, they sought to root politics in metaphysics – in other words, in a fundamental understanding of the nature of humankind and the end or purpose of life. This was later taken up in a religious context, with the idea that the right form of government was one that reflected the natural order itself, as created by God, establishing a mediaeval hierarchy for earth and heaven. But in Renaissance Italy, conflicts between city-states, and the intrigues of political life, suggested that there were occasions when cunning, rather than godly obedience, might prevail.

Thinkers here include: Plato, Aristotle, Augustine and Machiavelli.

The rise of the individual

Following the Reformation and the English Civil War, the seventeenth and eighteenth centuries saw the development of a very different approach to politics. This is the period in which the wishes of the individual became paramount, and political structures were justified on a basis of a Social Contract or agreement between individuals. Rights and freedoms were debated, the French had a revolution and the American colonies broke away from British control. The end of that period also saw the rise of utilitarianism (with political systems judged according to their ability to deliver the greatest benefit to the greatest number of citizens) as an ethical philosophy, and its parallel in the development of democracy. No longer asking what is the fundamental essence of humankind, the question shifts to 'How are we to decide how best to organize our society?'

Thinkers here include: Hobbes, Locke, Rousseau, Hume, Burke and Paine.

The evolution of systems

General systems of thought tend to create political philosophies as part of their overall understanding of reality. Kant, for example, produced rational principles for judging right and wrong, independent of anticipated results, inclinations or individual wishes. His famous 'categorical imperatives' – that something is only right if one could wish everyone else to adopt the same principle of action, that people should be treated as ends and never only as means, and that we should behave as though legislating for a kingdom in which everyone is an autonomous and free human being – have huge political implications. Hegel explored the idea that society was in a constant process of change, in a dialectical process, and Marx took that up and formulated his 'dialectical materialism' in which political change comes by way of class struggle. You also had the impact of Darwin and the idea of evolution through natural selection, and the attack on democracy by Nietzsche, who saw it as supporting the weak at the expense of the strong. And, at the other extreme, Mill develops the implications of utilitarianism, and argues for liberal values and freedom. By the end of the nineteenth century there was a huge range of political systems of thought.

Thinkers here include: Kant, Hegel, Marx, Mill and Nietzsche.

The twentieth-century clash of ideologies

The traumas of the twentieth century concern the clash of political ideologies that have deep roots in political philosophy. There is the massive rise and fall of Communism, the challenge of Fascism in Italy and Germany, and the steady global growth of democracy, riding on the back of capitalist economics. Anyone who is tempted to question the relevance of political philosophy need only contemplate the millions who died in that troubled century for the sake of political ideologies. But during much of that time political philosophy was in the doldrums. Like ethics, it came under criticism that normative judgements (saying that something is right or wrong) were meaningless, because they could not be justified on the basis of facts. Hence, for some years, much political philosophy simply explored the origins of political structures and the meaning of key terms, without working from normative first principles. There were exceptions, of course, including those mentioned below, who challenged ideologies.

Thinkers here include: Berlin, Hayek and Popper.

Later twentieth century and the dominance of liberal democracy

By the last three decades of the twentieth century, we have the progressive decline in socialism and communism and the dominance of the liberal democratic tradition. Political philosophy was revived, largely as the result of the work of John Rawls, whose seminal *A Theory of Justice* challenged utilitarian assumptions and re-instated normative philosophy to the political process. The rise of the feminist thinking questioned the male-dominated philosophy and politics of the past, and along with it the normative assumptions about the purpose of life and what constitutes fairness in society. There was also discussion about the scope of 'the political', the relationship of ideas to power, the nature of rights, the existential implications of politics and the need to explore new patters of work and living.

Thinkers here include: Rawls, Nozick, Dworkin, Habermas, Arendt, Foucault, Oakeshott, Sartre and Gorz.

Being selective ...

Political philosophy is not the same as the history of political ideas. An historical investigation requires pulling together all the evidence and seeing how things are related to one another, who influenced whom and so on. Philosophy is about ideas. So it is more important to select thinkers and get to grips with their ideas than try to cover absolutely everything that is said. This book is therefore selective in terms of the thinkers and arguments to be included, but endeavours to cover the main themes. This is particularly true of philosophers of the modern period, and those wanting to follow up in more detail might do well to start with the works of the thinkers mentioned above.

... and original

At the back of the book there is a brief list of suggestions for further reading, and this includes classic texts from the great thinkers of the past. However carefully one may summarize an argument, there is nothing quite like getting back to the original.

To read sections of Plato's *The Republic*, Machiavelli's *The Prince* or Locke's *Second Treatise on Government* is to be confronted with their ideas in the boldest way. If you want to discuss the place of education or family life, argue with Plato; if you feel that all politicians are out to maintain their own power, savour Machiavelli; if you are concerned with controlling the powers that should be given to a government, get into reading Locke. Dialogue with these thinkers is what counts when it comes to getting to grips with political ideas.

The agenda continues to change, and the twenty-first century has thrown up a whole new range of issues, from terrorism to global markets, to the power of the internet, to the environment. But first let us be clear about the function of political philosophy with regard to it ...

How do you decide what is right?

Any normative judgement (i.e. any judgement about what is right or wrong) needs to be justified with reference to something about which the person making the claim and those hearing it are agreed. If you say 'This is a good mobile phone', people are likely to know what you mean, because everyone is in broad agreement about what a phone should do. Does it work well? Do you get a good signal? Is it stylish? Does it have a built-in camera, MP3 player and so on? There can still be disagreements – one person would swap the MP3 player for longer battery life – but the fundamentals are not in question, because it is very clear what a phone is and what it does.

Things are not that straightforward with political philosophy. As we shall see in Chapter 02, the Ancient Greeks had views about the nature and purpose of human life, and so they were able to assess political ideas in terms of whether or not they could help people achieve their full potential as human beings. But what if there is no general agreement about what human life is for?

The 'social contract' approach gets around this problem by basing the political authority of the state on an agreement – either a literal one, or an implied one – between the people. In other words, people band together for their mutual benefit and decide the terms under which they will live. Even without an overall agreement about what people want, a democracy should enable at least a majority of them to have the government they think stands the best chance of reflecting their preferences.

In modern debates there are further levels of complication. **Post-modernism** challenges the idea that there can be a single 'right' way of seeing things, or that there is any established purpose in human life. If we want a sense of purpose, we have to provide it ourselves. But if purpose is contrived, how can it be used to give any objective justification of one political system rather than another. Without an objective measure, how can anything be 'better' than anything else? Added to this is another dimension, for in a *multicultural* society there is likely to be a variety of views and values, some of which may conflict with others. It is therefore increasingly difficult to find a common basis upon which to establish the necessary building blocks of certainty in political debates.

But even before the advent of post-modernism, there was a time – roughly from World War II through until the early 1970s – when there was general scepticism among philosophers about making normative judgements. In other words, they questioned whether moral statements could be shown to be true or false – and it was widely held that they were either the expression of one's emotions or approval (**emotivism**) or were recommending a course of action (**prescriptivism**). In either case, they lacked the sort of certainty and proof that science was offering in its description of the physical world.

During that period, the moral theory of **utilitarianism** (judging actions according to whether they offered the greatest benefit to the greatest number) tended to dominate political thinking. Economics and statistics can show what is actually happening in the political arena – and political ideas may therefore be assessed according to whether or not they deliver statistically-proven benefits to a majority.

But utilitarianism has its limitations, as was pointed out in 1971 by John Rawls. His 'thought experiment' that suggested that people could establish rational and logical rules for the distribution of resources, triggered off a range of debates, and exposed the dangers that, based on utilitarianism alone, it is difficult to see how minorities could be protected from the power of majorities.

But fundamental questions remain:
- How do you know what is right?
- On what basis can you decide the best way to conduct political life?
- How can you justify or effectively criticize a political system?

Some political philosophers (for example Michael White, in his *Political Philosophy: an historical introduction*), have argued that political philosophy needs to be grounded in a 'normative anthropology'. In other words, that there needs to be agreement on (or at least rational justification of) views about the value and purpose of human life. Without that, there is no solid foundation for political ideas. Other philosophers – whether from a post-modernist or a linguistic background – do not see that as essential. You may want to take your own view on this, after looking at the various arguments.

Justification, not just clarification

Some see philosophy's main task as clarifying concepts. That would imply that the task of philosophy is to look at the key ideas in political debate – freedom, rights, justice, democracy, and so on – and to examine what people really mean by them, and how they are related to one another. That is the sort of philosophy that clears the mind but does not necessarily change the world.

But there is another tradition of political philosophy. Marx famously declared that he wanted to change the world, rather than just interpret it, and many other political thinkers have impacted on the course of history. Rousseau's writings were to influence the French Revolution and Locke's the American Declaration of Independence. Nietzsche's work was read by Mussolini and Hitler (and sadly misused by them), and socialist ideas lay behind the setting up of the welfare state and health service in Britain. Today, neo-conservative views in the United States have influenced, among other things, American foreign policy with respect to the Middle East and the Iraq War. Discussions about terrorism and how to resist it are not just about words, but are desperately important in terms of security and human rights. So political concepts are not just there to be clarified, they need to be examined.

Political ideas are potent; but are they valid? The only way to establish that is by taking a two-stage look at them. First of all they need to be clarified: What exactly do we mean by fairness, or equality, or democracy? But secondly, they need to be justified: On what basis can you argue for the fairness of this or that political system? On what basis can you justify taking military action?

Like ethics, political philosophy is therefore concerned with the practical. It addresses issues of immediate concern to everyone and examines ideas that have – for good or evil – shaped the lives of whole generations. When some crucial event takes place – a war, an economic crisis, a global threat, a spate of terrorist attacks – people will naturally ask fundamental questions about how we should deal with such things. Politicians are required to find answers and implement them, but they need to be guided by principles about how we should live and how society should be governed. So circumstances are always throwing up new issues for political philosophy.

The modern agenda

Political philosophy has changed considerably during the last 40 years. Before the 1970s most political philosophy comprised of looking at constitutions, how they were justified and how well they served to benefit the lives of citizens. After that time, the focus tended to shift towards key concepts such as:

- freedom
- justice
- equality of opportunity
- rights
- fairness in sharing material resources
- political authority and security.

In other words, the focus went from looking at the political structures within which people live, to looking at those things that the individual might justly expect the state to provide or to facilitate.

But the problem is that these concepts may compete with one another. If everyone were given complete freedom, there might be no justice of fair sharing. If everyone were forced to be equal, and to receive a fixed share of material goods, individual freedom to improve your situation in life would be curtailed. What one person may see as justice and fairness, another may see as infringing his or her individual rights.

A key feature of political philosophy is negotiating between these principles, and getting them to interlock for maximum benefit. But 'maximum benefit' suggests some form of distributive justice – in other words, that society should be so organized that everyone receives a fair and appropriate share of resources. For some, that economic agenda remains central to the task of political philosophy.

But there are many other areas where principles conflict. On the one hand, people argue for freedom of the press, on the other for privacy for the individual. Are these compatible?

Privacy and press freedom

Both the Press Complaints Commission and European case law uphold the principle that people have a right to go about their business without be hounded by the press or paparazzi. Privacy is regarded as a right that applies equally to the relatively unknown person and the celebrity. On the other hand, celebrities deliberately put themselves in the public eye – that is what makes them celebrities. Does that imply that they have set aside their right to privacy? We may ask:

- Does the public have a right to know what celebrities are doing, simply because they are celebrities?
- Should the press be inhibited in its reporting, simply because it might be embarrassing for those who otherwise benefit from press attention?

Article 8 of the Human Rights Act, protects the right to family life (and therefore suggests that media intrusion should be restrained), while Article 10 gives people the right to know where there is a public interest.

How do you balance freedom of information against the right to privacy?

An example:

Media coverage of celebrity adultery may be trivial, but beneath the surface there can be serious issues of principle. For example, at the end of 2006, a sports personality managed to get an injunction against a man with whose wife he had been having an affair, preventing him from selling his story to the press. The grounds on which he obtained it were that such media coverage would inhibit the possibility of reconciliation with his wife.

The cheated-on husband, while free to tell friends and family what had happened, was not able to make it more widely known. There are two questions of principle here:

- Should it be made illegal for someone to tell their own story, on the grounds that it might adversely affect someone else? What about freedom of speech?
- Should the press have a right to expose celebrity adultery, if no genuine public interest is served by doing so?

With the twenty-first century there arrived issues that were not on the radar in earlier times. The last two decades of the twentieth century saw the progressive failure of socialist and communist regimes, leaving the United States as the sole superpower. Liberal democracy and capitalism seemed to have become the only viable political and economic option. Indeed Francis Fukuyama, in his book *The End of History and the Last Man* (1992) argued persuasively that there was a universal desire for the freedoms and benefits of modern western society, and this implied that the liberal-democratic view, in the form of individual freedom and free-market economics, would be the destination of choice for everyone. That view was reflected in the 'neo-conservative' agenda in the USA, which we shall need to consider later.

To some, there is nothing more to discuss – the old soviet-style planned economies have failed, labour and socialist parties have opted for the centre ground, and liberal democracy and free-market economics have triumphed. The sole criterion for political success is an ever-increasing standard of living and the provision of more and more consumer goods within secure national borders. If that is achieved, there is little for political philosophy to discuss – all that a government needs to do is adopt the policies that deliver on its economic promises.

But there are other huge issues to be addressed within the modern world. With global communication and economic structures, we have the issue of the relationship of individual nation states and international bodies. Post-colonial issues for the developing world, and multicultural ones in the developed world, both cut across the traditional national and cultural boundaries. These concerns include:

- civil rights
- feminist thinking

- globalization
- international responsibility – both in terms of war and the environment
- religious elements in political divisions
- climate change and political ecology
- terrorism.

These newer issues cannot be dealt with simply in terms of the older discussions between socialist and capitalist priorities. The rising threats to the newly-dominant, liberal-democratic view of society come from exactly those groups who reject the individual-centred philosophies of social contract and utilitarianism, handed down from the period of the seventeenth to nineteenth centuries, in favour of submission to a larger sense of purpose and meaning, whether religious or cultural.

Money and power are great motivators – for individuals and also for states – and a cynical manipulation of political goals in order to generate them, either for a ruler or a particular section of the population, is always going to be a temptation. Machiavelli took a wry look at the strategies for maintaining power in Renaissance Italy, and his comments remain relevant today. Politics can be a game to be played with high stakes by those fuelled by the power it offers.

Who offered what, when, on inheritance tax?

A spat between the British government and the Conservative opposition in October 2007 concerned inheritance tax. The Conservatives claimed that the government had only offered to reduce the liability for inheritance tax because they had promised to do so, if they came to power, at their Party Conference. The government insisted that its own plans to do so predated the Conservative promise.

Tax cuts are a great incentive when it comes to voting for one party or another. On the other hand, one person's tax cut is another's loss of social provision.

- How can a politician be completely objective about taxation levels in a politically competitive environment?
- Does tax inevitably provide an opportunity for a Machiavellian manipulation of figures and intentions?

But to the more profound question 'What is life for?' the suicide bomber, the aid worker and the venture capitalist may have very different answers. Political philosophy itself depends on establishing at least some basic answer to that question, for without that there is nothing to counter the accusations that money and power rule over reason and principle in the political sphere, and it makes little sense to discuss the rights and wrongs of political organizations and actions.

The structure of this book

Chapters 02 and 03 look at two broad periods of history: the first from Ancient Greece through to the Renaissance; the second taking in the seventeenth- and eighteenth-century developments in terms of the social contract and utilitarianism. Chapter 04 moves on to examine the ideas and ideologies that came to dominate the twentieth century – including Communism, Socialism, Liberalism, Conservatism and so on – while recognizing that their roots go back to the nineteenth century and beyond.

But since political philosophy is concerned with the key concepts, we shall look first at 'freedom', then 'equality and fairness', and finally 'rights, justices and the law'. Clarifying these concepts and seeing how they relate to one another is absolutely central for a good grasp of the subject.

But there are two perspectives that need special consideration. The first concerns the place of women in society. Most of the thinkers in the history of political philosophy have been men, and men have dominated political life. A feminist perspective is therefore essential. The second acknowledges that many – in fact, most – nations are now multicultural; some through immigration, but more generally from the global impact of commerce and communication. How do we achieve fairness and respect for individuals in a society where cultural values are varied? Should ethnic minorities maintain their own traditions, or should they conform to a national norm? At one end of the scale of answers to this question comes the desperately sad phenomenon of ethnic cleansing.

From Chapter 09 onwards, the book explores the position of the individual nation state in a world of multinational corporations, global markets and global threats. Sovereign states are no longer as sovereign as they were! Threats, whether from terrorism, war or climate change, respect no national boundaries.

The book then concludes with some observations and thoughts about the future of political philosophy, and offers a range of suggestions for further reading, including a list of classic texts.

Presenting the subject ...

Most books present an argument; they are written because the author feels that he or she has a particular point to make, or a gap in existing knowledge to fill. By contrast, this book seeks to present political philosophy itself *as a subject*.

Without trying to argue to any one conclusion, it attempts to open up the issues and set them in context, along with an agenda for the modern debate. If some questions appear rhetorical, or show political bias one way or another, that is the inevitable result of attempting to unpack and get to grips with the issues. Overall, it is left for the reader to draw his or her own political conclusions.

02

looking for the good life

In this chapter you will learn:
- about political thinking in Ancient Greece
- about Plato's ideal ruler
- why Aristotle aimed at the good life
- of mediaeval unworldliness
- of intrigues and dreams in the sixteenth century.

Some conception of what the 'good life' is about is fundamental to political philosophy. When people speak about fairness, or equality, or justice, they do so because they want people to be treated properly, and given the possibility of living well. The basic question for political philosophy is this: *What sort of political structure will enable people to live well?*

If we do not know what it means to live well, if we have no idea about those things that enable people to live life to their greatest possible capacity, then we have no hope or basis of assessing the political aspects of life – because politics is not an end in itself, but a means to an end, and that end is the 'good life'.

Why Ancient Greece?

Like so much else in Western philosophy, the agenda for later debates was set in Ancient Greece. There the fundamental questions were: 'How can we live the good life?' and 'How should we organize our civic life?' These were asked against a background of small city-states – some democracies, some oligarchies, some ruled by tyrants. Their world was very different from ours, but many of the issues with which they battled remain with us to this day.

One reason why it is important to take note of the political thinking of ancient Greece is that, within that society, political life was regarded as the necessary vehicle for achieving justice in society and, for each individual, a way of developing personal qualities or virtues. In other words, personal values and goals were to be expressed in the context of the *polis*, or city-state. Aristotle described man as a 'political animal', and the idea that an individual should not wish to be involved in civic life was unthinkable.

The Classical period of Greek political thought, represented by the work of Plato (428–348) and Aristotle (384–322), ran from the early fifth to the late fourth centuries BCE. By that time, Greece had established itself into about 750 self-governing city-states. Each *polis*, as these were called (from which we get the term 'politics') had its own particular form of government. Most were very small, many having less that 1000 citizens, but the largest – Athens – had 45,000 citizens. These *poleis* had been in existence for up to 400 years before the Classical period, so Plato and Aristotle were not devising some new theory of politics, but were putting together a logical justification for political structures that had been around for a considerable time. In addition, as we shall see, Plato in particular was trying to link the structures of political life to his overall view of the world, and of the place of reason within it.

The last 30 years of the fifth century BCE had been a time of considerable bloodshed and violence. The Peloponnesian War of 431–404 BCE came to an end with the defeat of Athens at the hands of Sparta, its democracy was overthrown and replaced by the rule of the Thirty Tyrants (which was backed by the Spartans, and led by Plato's cousin, Critas). Political opponents were executed, free speech was restricted and all who appeared to challenge or threaten the political status quo were punished. The Tyrants were overthrown the following year and democracy reinstated, but that did not imply total freedom of thought or speech – Socrates managed to survive the rule of the Tyrants, only to be put on trial and executed four years later for challenging established ideas.

It was not a time of idyllic peace and simplicity, but one that was as ruthless and unpredictable as any modern era.

Political life

Both Plato and Aristotle argued that the *polis* was needed because people were not self-sufficient, and that some things could only be achieved communally. At the same time, both felt that political life was a natural function of humankind – there is never a sense that one can opt to be a lone individual, separated off from others. And, if there was a major distinction to be made between nature (*physis*) and law (*nomos*), it was that the man-made laws should be rooted in the nature of humankind.

Political life was life in the *polis*. It was not a separate option for professional politicians, which the ordinary person (following a personal and economic agenda) took an interest in only when he or she was directly affected. Rather, political involvement was implicit in civilized living, not an optional extra, and Aristotle (*Politics*, 1.2.1253) said that the person who lived separate from a *polis* was either a beast or a god.

However, Athens was also concerned to protect individuals, allowing them basic freedoms and also giving them protection from undue interference from agents of the *polis*. But it was clear that individual citizens could only flourish if the *polis* within which they lived was stable and secure – all were bound together, with responsibilities towards the welfare of one another.

Political life was closely bound up with the idea of virtues. These were not simply private moral values, but those qualities without which it was not possible to live and flourish within a *polis*. The Athenians were therefore willing to define the qualities that made for a good citizen and people were encouraged to participate politically on the grounds that the *polis* provided the context for living the good life.

But Athenian democracy was quite different from modern representative democracy. First of all, neither women nor slaves could take part – which therefore eliminated a majority of the population. But secondly, it was conducted directly and immediately by those who were qualified, not by selected representatives – and that, of course, is why a majority of people could never have taken part, since they did not have the leisure to do so. But it is important to remember that Aristotle assumed that those who met at the public meeting would know one another, and that this would influence the way in which the debate was conducted.

The matters to be discussed and voted on in the public meeting were sorted out and proposed by a council. Members of that council were chosen by lot from among representatives from each of the local areas of the *polis*. Every free male was eligible for holding office in the *polis*, and most were chosen by lot, rather than by election. The only exception to this, in Athens, was for the posts within the army, for which a particular talent was necessary.

However, in general, it meant that everyone eligible would have an opportunity to take an active part in political life. Aristotle argued that, when citizens come together for the process of decision making, they are better collectively than any excellent individual might be. Hence there was respect for the give and take of argument, and the assumption that final decisions would be the better for it. Freedom of speech reflected the sense that all citizens were free and equal. The individual citizen was to think of himself as part of the *polis*, jointly responsible for its operation, not a private and autonomous agent who could opt for minimal political control. And, of course, the right to speak in the assembly, and to be considered an equal citizen, went along with an obligation to serve in the military and to defend the *polis*.

However, there were limits to free speech, especially when the *polis* felt that it was threatened by the views of an individual.

The most famous example of this was Socrates, who was condemned by a jury in 399 BCE for impiety (i.e. not recognizing the established gods of the city) and 'corrupting the young men' of Athens. This was an exception, however, and was seen as an example of the suspicion and fear at the end of the fifth century resulting from the trauma of the rule of the 30 Tyrants.

Necessary virtues

Protagoras – the first political theorist – was a sophist, whose thoughts are known through Plato's dialogue that is named after him. He offers a myth for the origins of politics – namely that when people gathered together to form societies, they generally failed because of human violence towards one another, but the gods provided two virtues to enable society to work:

- *Aidos* – moderation and respect for others
- *Dike* – justice.

Political wisdom, he argued, springs from these two virtues, which every citizen should possess, on pain of death, and which they should teach to their sons, and a city should use those with the most talent, without thereby denying that everyone else has something to contribute also. Moderation and respect for others lies behind the key idea of equality; justice – the term that Plato seeks to define in *The Republic* – is about how all can be treated equally and fairly.

Politics and ethics

Normative political judgments may be thought of as the social aspect of ethics, in that they make claims about how one *should* live in community. In studying ethics, there are two important and closely-related theories that originated together in the Greek period – 'natural law' ethics and 'virtue' ethics:

- The natural law approach was based on a conception of the essence of human life and therefore what was fundamental to human existence (e.g. the right to protect one's life if threatened).
- The 'virtue' approach was based on examining those qualities that enabled human beings to flourish.

If human beings are fundamentally 'political animals', as Aristotle suggested, then engaging in politics is absolutely natural, and attempting to live as an isolated individual is unnatural. Qualities such as respect for others and the quest for justice are therefore not arbitrary and optional extras, but express something fundamental to human life, something without which we are in danger of becoming sub-human.

Socrates is credited with saying that 'The unexamined life is not worth living', but it was equally true that – as far as qualified adult males were concerned – the un-political life was equally not worth living.

Notice how different this is from life in most modern democracies. The central features of life revolve around a person's family, friends and work. Unless they belong to the minority of political activists, or become involved in local politics, the political is something that they view on the TV, and assessed in terms of the benefit or otherwise that they receive from political institutions. Most are only marginally engaged, turning out to vote if the issues at stake are seen to impact on them personally.

Today, the economic benefits that the individual receives have become the baseline for evaluating political performance. Not so in Ancient Greece. With its slavery, the inferior position given to women, and its frequent readiness to go to war, it was not always a comfortable society in which to live, but it was one that established political engagement as the norm of civilized life.

Plato and the Good

Plato's political views are to be found in *Gorgias*, and in his late works, *The Statesman* and *Laws*, but by far his best-known work and the key to his philosophy is *The Republic*. This book, like his other works, is set out in dialogue form, with Socrates debating the nature of justice with a range of characters who represent the various political viewpoints. It is very readable, and touches on so many philosophical issues that it is an ideal starting point not just for a study of political philosophy, but for philosophy in general.

What is justice?

In the dialogue, various options are presented. The debate opens by Thrasymachus arguing that justice is whatever is in the interests of the stronger – a view that remains popular today, and leads ultimately to a cynical rejection of the whole political process. This is rejected in the dialogue by Socrates (through whose mouth Plato expounds his own philosophy). He recognizes the deeply selfish elements in human nature – as seen in the myth of the ring of Gyges. Armed with a ring that makes him invisible, Gyges seeks by intention what Oedipus achieved by accident, killing his royal father and sleeping with his mother – the ultimate Greek tragedy. Given the opportunity to behave with impunity, people will be selfish and bring about their own downfall. What Plato wants is to offer a higher vision of ethics and the political virtues.

Another argument, put forward by Glaucon, is that human nature needs to be restrained for the general benefit of society. In other words, there needs to be an agreement to prevent harm by restraining self-interest. In this, Plato anticipates the whole 'social contract' basis of political philosophy, but again he sees it as inadequate.

His own view comes in an extended exploration of the nature of the self and of the state. He points to the three aspects of human beings: the appetites, the spirit or directing element, and reason. His ideal for the human being is a situation where reason rules over spirit and appetite. And this, of course, links reason with his whole notion of the best form of life – if virtue and knowledge are one and the same, then a life ruled by reason will also be the most virtuous.

In the same way, he argues that there are three classes of people in the state: the workers (corresponding to the physical appetites), those whose role it is to defend the state (corresponding to the spirited element) and finally the philosophers (reason). He argues that justice is done when each part of society is treated correctly according to its nature, and hence – since an individual is best ruled by reason – the state should be ruled by Guardians who are trained as philosophers.

Plato is effectively trying to explain the value of justice to those, like Thrasymachus, who see it as an inconvenience, or as rules to be avoided if possible, in striving for the benefit of the self. What he tries to show, by making the analogy with parts of the self, is that justice is essential for human flourishing, even within the self, quite apart from its effect on other people.

In Books 8 and 9 of *The Republic* Plato sets out the dangers of promoting the spirited and appetitive aspects of humankind above that of reason. He criticized states that put courage above all other virtues – notably Sparta – since it needs to be tempered by a sense of moderation and kindly disposition towards others. He would not have thought much of modern military dictatorships, nor a society where most people are regarded only as politically docile consumers.

Virtue as knowledge

The key to Plato's political thought is his conviction that knowledge and virtue are one and the same. Whatever is reasonable is right; whatever is right is reasonable. He holds that injustice is caused by ignorance, and therefore the man of reason will always act justly. For Plato, philosophers have a reasoned understanding of reality – their right to rule derives from their understanding of reality, and of what is in the interests of all who live within the *polis*. They alone have a natural understanding of those ethical principles that make for human flourishing and the political structures within which it can come about.

The cave

In one of the most famous passages in all philosophy, Plato describes prisoners in a cave, chained to face a wall upon which shadows move to and fro, cast by objects being moved between them and a fire which burns behind them. Having known nothing else, the prisoners mistake the shadows for reality.

One prisoner is freed, and forced to turn to see the objects and the fire, and then – painfully – is forced up to the light beyond the cave. Having seen this, he recognizes the shadows for what they are, and is then required to return and explain that to the other prisoners, who reject his claims as foolish and continue to concentrate on predicting the patterns and movements of their shadows.

This analogy is generally used to highlight Plato's theory of knowledge – the difference between individual things (the shadows) and the corresponding eternal realities. But it is equally an account of the folly of political life. Those who concentrate on the passing shadows – trends, focus groups, opinion polls and the media in a modern context – are unable to appreciate the fundamental realities and principles that alone will bestow wisdom.

Hence, those who are to rule the state – the Guardians – need to be trained and equipped to do so in such a way that they do not fall into the temptations of impartiality and self-interest, but constantly use as their reference the sun beyond the cave – his 'Form of the Good'.

The sceptic asks …

Someone may claim to know 'the Good' and therefore to have the authority to rule, but how do you know? How can that claim be judged, other than by someone who has an equal knowledge of 'the Good'? And how can you know who is qualified to do that?

With no external means of judging a claim to knowledge, we slip down into modern **relativism** and **post-modernism** – a buffet of views to be sampled at will.

Scratch the surface of Plato's argument, and you might find that it leads to rule by an unchallengeable intellectual aristocracy.

Propaganda and censorship

In order to create the right conditions for the training of Guardians, Plato advocates censorship, since many of the classical tales present images of heroes that are ruled by their emotions and aggressive urges, and are far from good examples of the virtues he wants to promote.

Furthermore, he needs to propagate the 'noble lie' that people are naturally born into one of the three classes – the workers, the warriors, and those who are destined to rule. He wants to present this as a divinely ordained hierarchy, with each section of the population doing what it is created to do. People need such myths in order to keep them in their place.

This is an example of his tendency to see the good of the whole *polis* as taking priority over the rights of individual citizens, but that establishing *polis*-focused justice will, in the long run, also benefit every individual within it. Like much propaganda, Plato's is done for the best of intentions – to keep the lower orders comfortably in their place!

Training to rule

In order to produce his required Guardians, Plato proposes what amounts to a system of eugenics and the destruction of family life. Breeding is restricted to the healthiest and most athletic of the eligible age range, and their offspring are brought up and educated communally, so that they would have no knowledge of their particular parents, and thus avoid bias, regarding all those of an appropriate age as potentially their parents, and thus treating all with respect.

For reflection

Clearly, what Plato had in mind would go against what we would now see as the fundamental rights of both parents and children. But he was not describing an actual state, nor was he ever to be challenged to put his proposals for training the Guardians into practice. His argument is about what would be required to produce ideal rulers.

- To what extent are we prepared to accept fallibility and partiality in our rulers, given that they have not been selected at birth and trained for their role?

Plato also considers it important that rulers, as individuals, should be free from the temptation to accumulate gold or silver, for fear that, once they start to accumulate benefits from their office, they will turn into tyrants seeking their own advantage, rather than the good of the *polis*.

But for all the draconian measures that Plato seems to want to impose, his intention is not to promote politics or political power as such. Everything in *The Republic* aims at promoting the right conditions for its citizens: conditions that allow an ethical environment within which they can fulfil themselves.

His option

In *The Republic* Plato rejected various political options:

- Tyranny, because a single person, although perhaps initially representing and appealing to the ordinary people, may become corrupted by power.

- Timocracy (rule by the most powerful), because those who are in power because of their status are liable to be aggressive and more likely to declare war.

- Oligarchy (rule by a wealthy or privileged elite), because it is likely to encourage huge differences between rich and poor.

- Democracy, because it tends to anarchy.

In all these, he tries to balance the need for stability and insight into the best way to run society, with a recognition that people tend to go for what is in their own interests, and that most of these forms of government are in danger of favouring those by whose power they have been set up.

After the riots in Burma

Kevin Doyle, writing for the *Guardian* (13 October 2007), interviewed people in Rangoon following the repression of the pro-democracy demonstrations. Amidst the general sense of helplessness and the anti-government resentment, one man took a pragmatic line on the options which originally faced Plato:

'Democracy does not fit well in Burma, the generals are gangsters but at least they can run things. These democratic parties have no experience of running the country.'

- So what qualities make for a good leader? Is integrity and vision essential, or can it be trumped by experience and determination?

Plato's option, of course, is that the ideal state should be run by Guardians who are philosophers, motivated by insight and reason and immune from selfish concerns. But it is a curious feature of the Guardians that, when they are finally ready to take on the responsibility of running the *polis*, in the latter part of their lives and after their strict regime of education and training, Plato considers that they will do so only reluctantly, preferring the life of the philosopher to that of the ruler.

Conviction politicians

One tends to assume that those running for office in a democracy, or who rise up through the ranks to become a military dictator, achieve their position because of:

a) their desire for power, or
b) a genuinely altruistic desire to make a difference to people's lives.

An indifferent politician is a failure and an indifferent candidate is the least likely to be elected. Yet it is Plato's contention that such indifference to their own position of authority is a key feature of those best suited to rule.

Conviction politicians rally support and get things done; yet they can never be absolutely balanced in their judgement – for if they were, they would retain a degree of scepticism about their own 'convictions' that would undermine their position.

- Was Plato right in thinking that pure reason, unbiased and focused on eternal truths, is really what makes for a good and effective ruler?

The chief aim of Plato's republic is the production of excellence: breeding couples are selected for maximum quality of offspring and those born imperfect are left to die. It is a society ruled by a carefully groomed and trained elite. But however much the prevailing liberal-democratic sensibilities of the modern political world may find Plato's ideas offensive at times, they offer an interesting challenge.

Plato's system overcomes the danger that rulers will be elected on the basis of promises that they cannot keep, because they are based on a one-sided or biased view of the situation. If every ruler were free from family or other partisan ties, unconcerned about personal wealth or prestige, no doubt their choices would be the most wise and beneficial. *But would you want to live in a paternalistic society, where an intellectual elite condescend to stoop to organize the political regime along lines reasoned out with disinterested precision?*

Aristotle's political options

Aristotle's political philosophy is set out in his *Nicomachean Ethics* and *Politics*. In *Politics*, he asks why it is that political institutions come about in the first place. He recognizes the need for people to band together to help secure the necessities of life, but he considers that the state is one step beyond that, in that it is basically an association of kinship groups and villages who come together in order to establish a constitution that would allow them to live *the best life possible*. In other words, rather like utilitarian ethical arguments, people bind themselves to one another because they are looking for the greatest benefit for the greatest number, and find this in some form of political constitution, offering peace and a measure of protection.

For him, therefore, human beings are, by their very nature, political. His goal, *eudaimonia* (poorly translated as 'happiness', but really embracing the general sense of living and acting well), involved choosing to live as part of society. To reject society was to revert to the life of beasts. Only in participation can the individual fully realize his (not 'her' unfortunately – but we'll come to that later) potential.

Aristotle carried out a survey of the various forms of political organization to be found in his day and assessed their value. He was critical of those states where power was in the hands of one person (a tyranny) or a few people (an oligarchy), or even the rule of the mob, which is how he viewed democracies. He favoured those that were monarchies, aristocracies or polities. Although noting the difference between rule to a single person, a small number or by the majority, he also considered that it was more important to see *on whose behalf* the government operated. If on behalf of the majority of citizens, it met his approval; if on behalf of a minority or an elite, he saw it as perverted.

His last option – a 'polity' – describes a political situation where everyone can participate in the decision-making process, but only a few would actually take responsibility for ruling. His 'polity' came closer to what we would now think of as representative democracy, than does 'democracy', which implies rule by the whole *polis*. Like Plato, he had no illusions about the inability of the majority of people to make informed political choices. For Aristotle, man is both a rational and a political animal, and his aim (like that of Plato) is to apply reason to issues of political rule.

Natural law and politics

Aristotle initiated what is known as the 'natural law' approach to ethics. In other words, he argued that everything had a fixed nature and purpose within the world and that, once these were known, actions could be judged good or bad according to whether they contributed to or frustrated that purpose.

The same basic argument applies to politics. Aristotle assumed that the task of the state was to help people live well, and that meant helping them to fulfil themselves. His assessment of political systems therefore follows from his 'natural law' approach to ethics.

It is challenged – both in ethics generally and in politics – by those who argue that we do not have a fixed essence, but are free to set our own purposes and goals in life, and do not need to be told how to lead our personal 'good life' by anyone else.

Law and consent

At the end of *Nicomachean Ethics*, Aristotle points out that his intention has been to understand what is good, and thereby to make himself and others good. But he recognizes that most men are ruled by desires and needs rather than by reason. He therefore argues that laws are needed in order to guide them to become more virtuous – in other words, he seems to be saying that obedience to law becomes a necessary alternative to self-direction by reason, for those incapable of the latter.

Personal choice or legislation?

The fortieth anniversary of the 1967 Abortion Act sparked off discussion about whether the law on abortion in Britain should be revised. Some claimed that it was the right of the woman to choose whether or not to have an abortion. Others wanted to retain statutory control, both on the time limit for abortions, and also on the process by which the permission of two doctors is required. Should the government be expected to legislate on such personal issues, or should it be left to individuals to reason it out for themselves?

An Aristotelian natural law argument would suggest a balance between the right to life of the foetus, and the right of the mother to defend her own life and well-being, if it is threatened by the prospect of giving birth. That is an argument based on reason. The issue, however, is whether everyone is capable of making a mature and balanced judgement, or whether laws need to be framed to express what the 'reasoning' majority believe to be right.

A more stark version of the same issue is the rule applied in China a few years ago, forbidding couples to have more than one child.

• Should governments take a paternal view and legislate on personal matters, or should that be left to individuals, with governments doing no more that providing a secure framework within which freedom can operate?

In *Politics*, Aristotle criticizes militaristic states with imperialist intentions to increase their land and power, on the grounds that they actually undermine themselves, because they encourage similar traits in their citizens, who want to gain as much power and influence as they can. Hence they breed instability and discontent. This he contrasts with a state that allows and encourages freedom and participation, where citizens are willing to serve in the army to defend the state, on the basis that they feel they have a stake in it.

Aristotle thus argues for a partnership between ruler and ruled, recognizing that rule can be imposed on people for only so long before they will want to rebel. Hence, he is putting forward what amounts to a **consent-based** approach to government.

And that consent-based approach represents the balance between the potential anarchy of a direct democracy and the inflexibility of a rigid monarchy or military dictatorship. Such choices were very relevant in Aristotle's own day, and they remain so now. Stability in government depends on the consent of the people.

Natural subordination

Aristotle argued that some people were better suited to be ruled than to rule. In this category he placed both women and slaves, on the grounds that they did not reason well and would therefore be unable to rule themselves.

It was therefore appropriate that slaves should take orders, and he assumed that they would actually welcome the control of 'higher' beings, who would provide for them an ordered and purposeful life. In other words, if the slave cannot organize a proper life-plan, then someone else needs to do so – and thereby the master is enabling the slave to maximize his or her life, by performing a necessary function of rational control. Slavery actually meets the needs of the slave, not just those of the owner.

Aristotle considered the position of women to be rather different. He thought that they were quite capable of rational deliberation, but that they were not effective in applying reason to the process of living because they were overruled by their passions and emotions. They needed the rational guidance of men.

The argument used here is parallel to that used today in the case of children. Their reason is seen as immature, and therefore they need to be helped by those in authority over them (e.g. parents) in order to guide their progress.

Of course, it might be valid to ask of Aristotle whether his views are justified solely on the basis of his argument, or whether he was using his argument to justify a political and economic structure which was so deeply embedded in the society of his day that its overthrow would have been unthinkable.

Cynics, Stoics and Epicureans

After the Classical period of Plato and Aristotle, there was a shift away from making the politics of the city-state centre stage, and more towards the individual. Three groups of thinkers are relevant here: the Cynics, the Stoics and the Epicureans.

Diogenes of Sinope (400–325 BCE), most famous for sleeping in a barrel and having no more possessions than he could carry, rejected the conventions of social and political life, and was therefore called a 'cynic' – in other words, he was 'like a dog'. Until then, belonging to a *polis* was assumed to be essential – it gave you status, citizenship and protection. But Diogenes, when asked to which *polis* he belonged, replied that the world (*cosmos*) was his *polis*; hence he may be seen as the first 'cosmopolitan' man. That was a remarkable view to take at the time, although, to be fair, Diogenes probably presented it in rather a negative way, as rejecting the limitations of a single *polis*, rather than embracing it as a global citizenship. But it reflects a shift away from seeing the individual as part of the state, to seeing the state as an option imposed on an otherwise free individual.

The Cynics, in rejecting social conventions, were precursors of modern anarchists. They saw politics as, if anything, a hindrance to living the good life, and delighted in flouting the accepted norms of their day. Stoics, on the other hand (e.g. Seneca or Marcus Aurelius) tended to be more moderate in their views, although maintaining the value and significance of the individual.

The Stoics taught that one should live in conformity with the *logos*, or rational principle within everything. In this, they were not far removed from Aristotle's view that everything had a purpose or 'end', and that its good came in fulfilling itself. Some, like Zeno (332–265 BCE), tended to side against conformity to laws, while others, like Cicero (106–43 BCE), were more concerned to argue for balance and the need for people to work together for the common good. But politically they emphasized the individual, and his or her personal integrity. In particular the *Meditations* of Marcus Aurelius (121–80 BCE), although a set of personal reflections rather than a systematic work of philosophy, give the most direct insight into the Stoic view, and in particular the view of someone who achieves high political office – in his case, Emperor.

The other group of thinkers to mention here are the Epicureans. They held that the world was an impersonal place, indifferent to human welfare, and that it was up to individuals to seek their own happiness. Their tendency was to find this in simplicity of living, rather than extravagance, and they gathered together to share a communal life with those of similar view.

Although fascinating, there is no scope here to explore the thinking of these groups; they are mentioned only to make a single point – that even among the thinkers of Ancient Greece and Rome, there was a choice between the more centralized view of politics and the more individualistic. *Does the state exist for the sake of the individual, or the individual for the sake of the state?*

Mediaeval otherworldliness

In political philosophy, it may be tempting to jump straight from the work of Plato and Aristotle to the seventeenth- and eighteenth-century thinkers (like Hobbes and Locke) whose ideas have been directly influential on modern political developments. However, there are two other perspectives that need to be taken into account – one is the impact of the

Christian religion on political thought, and the other is the revival of the small-scale political entity in the cities of Renaissance Italy.

The religious perspective is well illustrated by St Augustine's *City of God*. Augustine (354–430) made the clear distinction between the worldly city (the City of Man) and the heavenly abode of the faithful (the City of God). His argument was that people live in two worlds, with two sets of commitments, but that the earthly ones were of little value when compared to the heavenly. Therefore, for the devout, they should not set great store by politics, and the only function they required of the state was that of protection – although even that was doomed to failure, because sinful human nature always led to strife.

One of the key questions, therefore, during the mediaeval period was the relationship between the Church and the state – between heaven and earth. It was believed that God had ordered and established society, and provided for it to be guided by the Church. Hence the devout were expected to accept the established secular authorities. The divine right of kings was part of that structure – the king ruling by the authority of God. It is also important to recognize that, as far as Europe was concerned, the Church had an authority that transcended the particular nation or monarchy. Rather than political authority being established by and for the people, you have authority being handed down from above – from God, via the Church and its approved secular rulers, to the people.

However, when we look at some features of that period (e.g. the Crusades) we find that spiritual goals were based on solid social and economic foundations, and that the various conflicts over power and authority were not so different from those of later times. The declared spiritual goals frequently masked the real political aims, and intrigue was found equally in Church and state.

In the thirteenth century the writings of Aristotle were once again being studied, taught in newly-established universities, and intellectual life was able to question political and religious authority. Seeking to combine the philosophy of Aristotle with Church teaching, Thomas Aquinas (1225–74) took a positive view of politics and law, because he believed that God had provided humankind with reason, and permitted secular authority to act on his behalf. However, the law should be 'natural law' – in other words, based on nature as interpreted by reason – and if the secular law was at odds with natural law, then the latter should take precedence. Thus the hierarchy was clearly established that the Law of God took precedence of the laws of man.

Overall, however, Aquinas took a more positive view of the secular realm than did Augustine. He even argued that the discipline of obeying the law, even if only from fear of punishment, had value, as it could lead both to peace and to the development of virtue.

Historical interest only?

Not at all. In the twenty-first century we have international terrorist organizations – including, of course, al-Qaeda – that follow a fundamentalist ideology that is both religious and political. In mediaeval Europe, someone might be required to obey the laws of their particular country, but was aware of a higher responsibility towards the laws of God, as interpreted by the international organization of the Church. In the same way, there are radical Islamist groups today who challenge people to set what they interpret as the requirements of *jihad* (divinely sanctioned struggle) above their duty to obey the laws of the land. *The issue of the relationship between religious and political allegiance continues to be relevant.*

Renaissance realism

For an utterly different approach to political philosophy, we may turn to a writer whose cynical observations of the power politics of Renaissance Italy, led his name to become synonymous with political intrigue – Niccolo Machiavelli (1469–1527).

Having spent his life in the political circles of his native Florence, close to the seat of power, Machiavelli wrote *The Prince,* which appears to be a handbook for the aspiring leader – setting out the best policies for holding together a state and increasing its power and authority. He shows that there are times when a ruthless but decisive ruler is more effectively able to control and benefit a nation than a more gentle but indecisive one.

Machiavelli is readable and stimulating, and he has that unusual quality of combining a serious and reasoned argument with wry observations of actual life and situations. How far he was making serious suggestions, and how far irony was his main weapon, is a matter for debate; his lively mind is not. *The Prince* is a great book of political philosophy, because it sets out its goals, looks at what is required to fulfill them, and then looks at the principles involved in doing so. It is realistic, rather than utopian.

In terms of political philosophy, Machiavelli sees maintaining the security and integrity of the state as paramount. All else in terms of ethical or political theory takes second place. If it is necessary to be harsh, cruel even, in order to maintain security, Machiavelli sees it as the right thing to do.

In particular, Machiavelli's advice requires that a ruler should be flexible, and should learn to anticipate the actions of others and respond accordingly. In particular, his view is one that is always pragmatic – know what you seek to achieve and then find the most effective way of achieving it. When others are crafty, adherence to absolute moral or political principles is a hindrance to maintaining one's position.

... or principled dreaming?

While Machiavelli was plotting success in Italy, Sir Thomas More (1478–1535) was rising through the English political ranks to become Lord Chancellor to Henry VIII. As a scholar and humanist, he was a very principled man, and paid for it with his life – for, having opposed the king's right to make himself head of the Church in England, he was executed for treason.

His *Utopia* is a wonderful book which, in fictional form, tells of an account of a far-off island, named Utopia, and established that name as a term for a social and political ideal. On the island of Utopia, small self-governing cities trade with one another and people only work as much as is needed to provide the necessities of life. All are equally responsible for getting work done and, with no hangers-on in the form of priests or aristocrats, each person's share of work is modest. All, both men and women are equal, and gold and silver are treated as worthless, thus avoiding avarice and economic competition, but allowing public heaps of gold to be used to pay mercenaries to take care of external defence.

In many ways it is a vision of a socialist state, utterly different from the Tudor monarchy, but Moor insists on standing back from what could be seen as political proposals. What he sets down is simply an account of what has been described to him about a far-off place, and he comments that some of the ideas appear strange, even ridiculous.

Machiavelli's *The Prince* was written in 1514, and More's *Utopia* in 1516. Both are enjoyably readable books, from minds that sought to make sense of the political intrigues, possibilities and principles of their day. They raise political questions that are still relevant and which form an interesting historical backdrop to the flurry of new political philosophy that arose in the seventeenth and eighteenth centuries.

Balance still needed

The balance between utopian and Machiavellian approaches – in effect, between idealism and realism – is still necessary if political ideas are to be credible. This is illustrated by the following quotation from *The Audacity of Hope* (Cannongate, 2007) by a democratic candidate for the US Presidency, Barack Obama. He speaks of those ordinary citizens who have grown up amidst the political battles, but have found their own way to make peace with their neighbours and with themselves:

'I imagine they are waiting for a politics with the maturity to balance idealism and realism, to distinguish between what can and cannot be compromised, to admit the possibility that the other side might sometimes have a point. They don't always understand the arguments between right and left, conservative and liberal, but they recognize the difference between dogma and commonsense, responsibility and irresponsibility, between those things that last and those that are fleeting.'

Distinguishing between the lasting and the fleeting is, of course, exactly what Plato was on about with his analogy of the cave.

03 the social contract

In this chapter you will learn:
- about the principles that established modern democracy
- why Hobbes thought a strong ruler was necessary to prevent chaos
- why Rousseau allowed a tyranny
- about controlling executive power.

In September 2007, pro-democracy demonstrations in Burma were ruthlessly put down by the military junta. Its actions were widely condemned, and commentators spoke of the military as acting against the wishes of the people. To take the most ruthless example, Stalin ruled the Soviet Union by terror: people were not free to challenge or question the state; dissidents were sent to the camps, or were killed.

There is no doubt that Stalin was firmly in control of the Soviet Union, and at the time of writing the military are firmly in control of Burma. But the question is: Should they be? By what right do governments or dictators rule? People may be controlled by threats and held in check by fear, but is that a legitimate exercise of political authority?

- When is it right for people to change an established political system (as happened in Eastern Europe, leading to the break-up of the Soviet Union)?
- When is it right for one nation to seek regime change in another, claiming to do so for the benefit of its people (as the US did in launching its attack on the regime of Saddam Hussein in Iraq)?

You can only get answers to those questions once you decide by what authority a government can rightly be established.

A related question is the authority a state should have over its citizens: *Why should we obey the government and its laws?* Do we do it on the basis that the government had a mandate to rule, because its party received the largest share of the vote? Do we do so on the more pragmatic basis that, if the laws of a state did not exist and command respect, the country would fall into a situation of anarchy, leading to mutual harm and mistrust? Or do we obey simply on the basis that we will be punished if we don't?

And at what point should we be free to reject and replace that government if it appears to be going against our wishes? Is a government to be judged on a utilitarian basis – that it produced the best result for the greatest number of people – even if it does not produce the best result for me as an individual?

But of course, there is a difference between power and authority. Anybody can force someone to do something by threatening to use power against them. But that does not mean that the person has 'authority' to do so. *Authority implies agreed legitimacy.* A law or an action is politically authoritative if, and only if, it has the backing of a legitimately established government, and one way of establishing that legitimacy is to base it on an agreed contract made between people and their rulers – the Social Contract.

Contracts, dilemmas and war games

In the 1950s, with the opposing nuclear arsenals of the USA and the USSR, there developed a 'Cold War' in which the theory of nuclear deterrence ensured that neither side would attack the other on the basis that the other had sufficient weapons in reserve that they could strike back with devastating consequences. The MAD (Mutually Assured Destruction) threat was seen as the way of ensuring that neither side would attack the other.

But the thinking behind that kind of strategy came from 'game theory', and one of the most significant of such games is known as 'the Prisoner's Dilemma.'

The situation:

Two prisoners are arrested and both are charged with two crimes – a lesser one for which there is sufficient evidence to find both guilty, and a more serious one for which conviction will only be secured if one of them agrees to confess.

The offer (made to each prisoner):

• If you confess to the more serious crime, you will receive a very light sentence, but your co-accused will serve the maximum sentence.
• If you *both* confess, you will each receive a sentence that is less than the maximum, but greater than the light one you will receive if you alone confess.
• If neither of you confesses, you will receive the maximum sentence for the lesser of the crimes. (i.e. more than if you alone confess to the more serious crime, but less than if you both confess to it).

The assumption of this dilemma is that each prisoner is self-interested and therefore not concerned with the sentence that the other will receive. What should they do?

The dilemma here is one of trust. If they agree that neither will confess, each will receive the more modest sentence. On the other hand, if one confesses, but the other does not, he will receive the lightest sentence, at the expense of the other. *But*, the problem is that each knows *the other has the same choice*. Each could go for trying to get the minimum sentence at the expense of the other.

Going for self-interest is not always straightforward. If you think the other person will keep his or her promise, you could cheat on your side of a bargain, and thereby gain an advantage. On the other hand, you know that the other person will be reasoning in the same way, and may therefore be equally tempted to cheat on you. How do you resolve this?

Trust and contracts

Faced with potential conflicts and mistrust, the best options might seem to be to make an agreement together for mutual protection and support, or to give full authority to an agreed ruler or judge. Both of these imply a contract: the first between citizens of a state, the second between each citizen and the chosen government or ruler.

The idea of the political contract has a long history. In his dialogue *Crito*, Plato puts forward the argument that, by choosing to live in Athens and accepting its protection and the benefits it offers, one is obliged in return to obey its laws. He has Socrates argue that, if a person does not want to obey the laws in Athens, he should go and live elsewhere.

But the renewed interest in contract came about because, with the new thinking produced during the Renaissance, and the upheavals in Europe caused by the Reformation, there emerged a society in which emphasis was increasingly placed on the individual. Rather than seeing society as a God-given structure within which individuals were required to fit, thus fulfilling their purpose within the whole, there was a view that people should be able to get together and take their own responsibility for the political rules under which they should live.

Thus we arrive at seventeenth- and eighteenth-century **contractarianism** – in other words, the attempt to find a rational justification for the modern nation state, based on the agreement of the people. This period set the foundations of modern democracy and liberalism – and thus forms the basis of modern political thought.

Key questions to ask about representation and consent are:

- Does this government represent me fairly?
- How do I give (or withhold) my consent for it to act in my name?
- Am I considered to have given my consent to a nation's political system simply by being born there? If not, at what point am I asked for my consent?
- What if I am a minority and all political decisions are made in favour of the majority? Does that mean that I will never be treated fairly (from my perspective) in a democratic system?

Today, most people favour some form of democracy – that people should agree together to support a government, rather than having one imposed on them. That has come about, to a considerable extent, through the work of thinkers who supported the idea of a social contract – including Hobbes, Locke and Rousseau.

Hobbes: an alternative to chaos

When a nation restricts civil liberties or the free-flow of information in the name of security, when it become defensive, when it insists on maintaining tight border controls to defend itself against terrorist threats or illegal immigrants, or when it claims absolute authority, it follows a line of reasoning that goes back to Thomas Hobbes (1588–1679).

Hobbes wrote at the time of political conflict – the civil war in England, the challenge to royal authority, the execution of Charles I and the setting up of the Commonwealth. Hobbes favoured the Monarchy, and was forced to flee to France in 1640. His best-known work, *Leviathan* (1651) – the title of which refers to the state, named after the great beast in the Book of Job, whose magnificence quelled all questioning – reflects his support for the authority of the monarchy. The charge against the king, at his trial in 1649, was that he claimed 'an unlimited and tyrannical power to rule according to his will, and to overthrow the rights and liberties of the people of England.'

So the key question for Hobbes concerned how and why a government is established, and what authority it should be given.

Understandably perhaps, he held a rather bleak view of human life and of the potential of society to descend into chaos and bloodshed. Most human behaviour is motivated by desires that lead to conflicts of interest and therefore disputes. He assumes

that mutual agreement alone would not be sufficient to settle
such disputes, unless there were to be some overall authority to
enforce compliance.

Therefore, the only hope for protection in a dangerous world is
to band together, to set up a powerful ruler or government, and
to agree to be committed to its authority. Failure to secure such
an authority leaves people vulnerable to a basic trait of human
nature, namely that everyone is going to be out for him/herself.
In such circumstances, few will have the trust required for
projects, like trade and education, that require cooperation. He
famously described life for humankind in its natural state as
'nasty, brutish and short', lacking all that makes for civilized
living, trade, learning and so on. And just as, in the earlier
'natural law' approach, the first natural right of every human
being is self-preservation, so the first duty of the state is to
protect against threats to life, both internal and external.

State power is legitimized by being set up by the agreement of the
people, for their mutual support and protection. The key thing to
appreciate about Hobbes's main argument, however, is that
authority is *given* to the ruler, rather than just *loaned*. Individual
wills are given up in favour of the single sovereign will.

But the problem with this is that, once set up between
individuals, the sovereign power does not have an *on-going*
agreement with each of the citizens, but has absolute and
unchallengeable authority. Of course, given Hobbes's
background, that would seem perfectly reasonable, for once the
sovereign power is open to challenge, each and every citizen
may start to doubt its authority and refuse its laws – and you
are back on the slope down to anarchy and civil strife.

Power and authority

Power is the ability to do something; authority is the right to do it.
A military junta may have the power to repress its people,
maintaining control through fear, but that does not mean that they
have the *right* to do so. To have authority requires that power is
acknowledged by the general consent of the people. And that, of
course, is the purpose of a social contract. Only with
acknowledged authority is it possible to settle disputes without
the need to resort to brute force.

On the other hand, to have authority without power makes a
government vulnerable, and denies it the ability to perform what
Hobbes saw as its primary purpose, namely security.

The main argument against Hobbes is that his social contract does not make a government sufficiently accountable for its subsequent actions. But he adds one qualification, to use his phrase, 'except where my life is threatened'. This would suggest that, in extreme circumstances, authority is not simply *given*, but is *loaned* and the condition of that loan is that the government provides security. Given that Hobbes's whole purpose is to establish an authority that proves security and avoids anarchy, this is reasonable. Hobbes allows people to rebel, but only if absolutely necessary in order to protect themselves.

Locke and the principles of democracy

John Locke (1632–1704) welcomed the 'glorious revolution' of 1688, when William of Orange arrived in England to establish a constitutional monarchy, and James II emigrated to France, thus showing that it was possible to remove and replace a ruler without bloodshed or national trauma, in stark contrast to the upheavals of the Civil War earlier in the century. His *Second Treatise on Civil Government* (1689) was a justification of that new political situation – a triumph of compromise that would establish a monarchy and strong leadership, but allow control to remain in the hands of the people.

In Locke's work we find much that has contributed to the modern liberal democratic tradition, and his ideas were to influence both the French and American constitutions. The reason why Locke is crucial in political philosophy is that he argued for representation in government, with ways of ensuring that governments are held to account.

Key to Locke's argument is that a government should establish laws by consent of the people, and should then be held accountable, so that no ruler can be *above* the law. Hence the institutions of government are agencies for the implementing of law, rather than having absolute power to make and change the law. This is what distinguishes Locke's position from that of Hobbes.

Locke was not as negative as Hobbes concerning the natural state, allowing that people could work together for mutual support and allowing them freedom, but he believed that such a state did not give protection for a person's 'property':

This makes him willing to quit this condition which, however free, is full of fears and continual dangers; and it is not without reason that he seeks out and is willing to join in society with others who are already united, or have a mind to unite for the mutual preservation of their lives, liberties and estates, which I call by the general name – property.

And when there were disputes:

Firstly, there wants an established, settled, known law. Received and allowed by common consent to be the standard of right and wrong, and the common measure to decide all controversies between them ...

Secondly, in the state of Nature there wants a known and indifferent judge, with authority to determine all differences according to established law.

Second Treatise of Civil Government, Chapter IX

Property

Locke saw that, in a state of nature, people could hunt animals and gather food, and thereby take for themselves what would previously be regarded as common. Their act of hunting had made it theirs, and they should therefore be entitled to it. He thus established the principle that the act of labour – mixing one's own efforts with what nature provides – is the basis for property.

Though the earth and all inferior creatures be common to all men, yet every man has a 'property' in his own 'person.' This nobody has any right to but himself. The 'labour' of his body and the 'work' of his hands, we may say, are properly his. Whatsoever then he removes out of the state that nature has provided, and left it in, he hath mixed his labour with it, and joined to it something that is his own, and thereby makes it his property.

Second Treatise ... Chapter V

For Locke, people are essentially free to take their own interests seriously; they have a right to work for and keep wealth, and if they have invested their time and energy in a project, even one that has taken natural resources that might originally have been considered to belong to everyone, then they are entitled to keep them for themselves. This right to own and defend one's property is a central feature of the freedom of the individual; the state is there to protect private interests, and to create the conditions of security that allow commerce. Naturally, the organization of defence and law requires raising funds through taxation, but Locke argues that this should be with the consent of the majority.

Whose land is it?

If, as Locke argued, the earth was common to all, and made into 'property' by being mixed with a person's labour, who really owns it?

The Chagos islands are in the middle of the Indian Ocean. They were first populated in 1776 by slaves from Senegal, Mozambique and Madagascar, brought to the islands by French colonists. But the British ruled the islands from the early nineteenth century, and their inhabitants eventually became British citizens.

But in 1966 the British government leased the main island (Diego Garcia) to the US for the construction of a huge air base, evicting about 2000 people from their homes and forcing them to leave the island and move to Mauritius or the Seychelles.

In 2004, the High Court ruled that their expulsion was unlawful, but the British Government still banned them from returning home. Finally in May 2007, they won the right to return to what they consider to be their 'motherland'.

- So who actually 'owns' Diego Garcia?
- Should it be owned at all?
- When a piece of virgin land (or in this case an archipelago of 65 coral islands) is occupied, should it, as Locke argued, become the 'property' of those who work to make it their home?
- From the sixteenth to the nineteenth centuries, European countries acquired an extensive portfolio of colonies throughout the world. Did they therefore 'own' those countries?
- When newly-arrived colonists encounter an indigenous population, who has the right to the land?

Laws and executive power

Locke also distinguishes between the legislative and executive aspects of government. The legislative side establishes the laws by which the state will be run. The executive sets about implementing them, and part of that implementation is the setting up of an impartial legal system. Hence the right of parliament to endorse or hold to account a government, and if necessary to change it. This remains an essential part of modern representative democracy. In Britain, the Prime Minister and other ministers are required to present themselves before the House of Commons to explain their actions and their proposals for legislation – and these can then be scrutinized and, if appropriate, changed, before they can become law.

Majority rule

How do you protect a minority or an individual from the wishes of the majority? And how do you establish that everyone has given consent to be governed in this way? Locke himself recognized this issue and made a distinction between consent that is given directly, in the making of an agreement, and consent that is *tacit*. Naturally enough, most people will be judged to have given tacit consent, since they have not actually been present to set up the government in the first place.

If rule is by consent, then I should be able to select and direct those who are set up to control me. But the laws are set up by the consent of the majority. How does an individual or a minority respond when the will of the majority – or at least, the government for which a majority has voted – goes against their own interests?

This may be termed 'the paradox of sovereignty': that people are subject to a ruler who is actually selected to act as their own agent.

Beware politicians bearing gifts ...

An example of this problem is seen every time there is a general election in the UK (and probably elsewhere also). When it comes time to be elected, the government, seeking a further mandate from the people, makes promises to the people about what they will do for them. In other words, it asks to be given authority, and therefore needs to promise to do what will be most popular. A government that promised nothing would hardly be expected to be voted into office. How can governments be honest about the tough or unpopular actions they might need to take, if they have to pitch their offer to the people in this way?

There is another fundamental problem here. The whole reason for establishing a social contract was that people, left to their own devices, could not always be trusted to keep their own contracts with one another, and hence that everyone would be vulnerable to exploitation by all the others. How then can people be trusted to keep the social contract they make with the government?

The logical answer to this is that they can't. If a small number of people defy the law, they may be punished for it. If a majority complain that a law is unjust, or seek to change the government, the fact that they are a majority appears to give their action legitimacy.

Representative democracy

From simple democracy in Ancient Athens, we have moved to a situation of representative democracy, necessitated by the sheer number of people involved. Hence it is clear that if representatives are to be voted into office, those voting must have a clear idea of what they will intend to do, to ensure that they will reflect the wishes of voters.

This is made more complex by the party system. Where the person standing for election belongs to a party, it is assumed that he or she will follow that party's position on the major issues under discussion. From time to time, of course, in order to represent constituents, a representative may need to go against the party line. But that is the exception rather than the rule.

Britain's two per cent effective democracy

Britain has a representative democracy, which suggests that everyone's vote counts. However, with a first-past-the-post system (in which each constituency elects its own representative on the basis of a simple majority, with no account being taken for the number of votes given to the other candidates), the results in most constituencies are a foregone conclusion. The final result, in terms of a balance of parties in the House of Commons, depends on some 900,000 (two per cent) of voters who happen to live in marginal constituencies, whose swing will decide the final result. Political parties therefore tend to pitch their offer to the 'middle ground', since that is where the final decision rests.

However, a system of proportional representation tends to give a more balanced, but less decisive result, with hung parliaments and governments being formed of more than political parts and therefore inherently unstable. We therefore face a familiar dilemma:

- Do you go for fairness, even if that makes the decision-making process more difficult?
- Or do you go for a pragmatic way of achieving a decisive result, even if most people are, in effect, disenfranchised?

It is assumed that, where a government is formed from those of a particular party who have gained a majority of seats, that government will put into effect those things that the party presented to the electorate in its campaign. Hence the government may claim to have a mandate from the electorate to put into effect the manifesto or platform upon which it campaigned.

But notice the problem this causes. In a representative democracy, only a majority of elected members need support the party which seeks to put itself forward to govern. Hence, at any one time, the government in power can, at the very most, claim to be implementing ideas voted for by a majority of the people, and it is more likely that, for any one particular piece of legislation, it will represent only a minority view. The democratic process itself cannot therefore give any guarantee to deliver a straightforward majority approval of any one piece of legislation.

It is also clear that, in any representative democracy which is organized along party lines, decisions about those things that fall within the responsibility of the executive, will (through a natural desire to stay in power) reflect the interests of the ruling party. This would include, for example, the decision about when to call a general election. In other words the consent and mandate of the people, which alone legitimizes those in office, can itself be timed to benefit those presently in office.

Will he, won't he?

In late September/early October 2007, during the conference season for the British political parties, there was much speculation about whether the new Prime Minister, Gordon Brown, would call an early general election. In the end, he didn't.

Political parties represent different groups of people within a democracy. To be fair, a democratic process should favour all equally. But a sitting Prime Minister can call an election as and when the polls suggest that (in the to and fro of political life) the presently ruling party stands best chance of being returned to power.

- Is that fair? Does it not mean that the election process is always biased in favour of the existing party of government?

There are other questions to be asked about political parties within a representative democracy, in particular concerning the requirement that MPs vote along party lines on some issues, rather than according to their individual judgement of the particular interests of their constituencies.

- Does the party system over-simplify political issues, by giving people a crude choice between parties, rather than expecting individual representatives to be responsive to their particular wishes?

To what extent, then, should a representative democracy with a party system claim to be able to put into effect a government which accurately represents the people? And if it admits the limitations of any such process, is there any better way of operating?

Might it be possible, for example, to hold a referendum on major issues? The problem here is that the framing of the straightforward question that it puts to the electorate in a referendum is in the hands of the government – and the way the question is framed may influence the result. Hence, with the best will in the world, the process of democracy is no more than an on-balance probability that the government is putting into effect the wishes of the people.

Key question: If a government is elected on a mandate, and the circumstances that led to the formulation of that mandate change, is that government entitled to act differently from the way it promised the electorate? That might appeal to common sense. On the other hand, if it then acts against its own mandate, does it not become an elected dictatorship – acting against the expressed wishes of the voters?

> **'Twas ever thus!**
>
> David Hume, commenting on the British balance of power between the Monarch, the House of Commons and the House of Lords, suggested (in his essay *Idea of a Perfect Commonwealth*, 1741) that peers should be made for life and not hereditary. The Lords should be elected and no commoner should be allowed to refuse a seat in the Lords if offered it. He sees an effective House of Lords as a good corrective to the possible whims of the sovereign and the power of the Commons. The effect of such reforms would be that:
>
> > 'By this means the House of Lords would consist entirely of the men of chief credit, abilities, and interest in the nation; and every turbulent leader in the House of Commons might be taken off, and connected by interest with the House of Peers.'
>
> More than 250 years later, Hume's comments are still relevant, although whether turbulent leaders of the Commons are mellowed by becoming Lords is a matter of debate!

Rousseau: the tyranny of the General Will

If people were not so foolish as to walk around brandishing the latest mobile phones and i-pods, there would be far less street crime, because the temptation to snatch and run would be diminished!

In essence, that was the view of Jean-Jacques Rousseau (1712–78) a philosopher and man of letters, whose personal life was remarkably colourful, and whose political and social views were to influence the French Revolution (even though he himself did not live to see it). He contrasted the natural state with the very unnatural conditions of society. In their natural state people would simply take what they needed for life, they would not be tempted to steal from others because the whole notion of private property would not exist. It is the privatizing of things that leads to social unrest.

Nevertheless, people do in fact live in society and are open to the corruption that comes with it, so how then might they regain their freedom and innocence? Are freedom and civil society compatible?

That, in effect, is the question that lies behind one of the great 'one-liners' of political philosophy, the opening of his book *The Social Contract*:

Man is born free, and everywhere he is in chains.

In *The Social Contract* he seeks to reconcile freedom and authority. He argues that one is obliged to obey the state because it represents the General Will – not just the will of the majority, but what everyone would *really* want, from a moral point of view, if they considered the situation rationally and took into consideration the interests of all.

Rousseau considered that, if you are enslaved by a particular interest or desire, you are not truly free, even if you are allowed to follow it. Freedom means freedom also from your own inclinations and passions. Hence Rousseau could accept that, in order to be truly free, people should obey the General Will, rather than following their own untrustworthy particular wills. If everyone were wise enough, they would see that true interest and fulfilment would come by following the General Will.

But here comes the catch. People are not always wise. They may not appreciate that the General Will represents their own best interests. They may not appreciate that following the General Will is their path to true freedom. Therefore it may be necessary for the state to force people to do what they would 'really' (if they were wiser) want in the first place. To use Rousseau's chilling phrase, they should be 'forced to be free.'

Back to Plato

Plato argued that philosophers should rule, since they alone were able to appreciate the eternal realities, rather than the passing shadows of everyday existence. Using a 'noble lie' if necessary, the lower orders would be kept in their place – which would be for their own good and the good of the city-state as a whole.

What Rousseau presents in the General Will, is not so different – what those who govern the state deem to be in the interests of all, will be imposed on all, since it is in their own best interest.

One real problem with Rousseau's approach is that it assumes that everyone wants the same thing – in other words, that the General Will represents the self-interest of all – and that it is a moral and political obligation of every citizen to follow that imposed self-interest. But:

- the first is, factually, impossible to establish (unless you can have a vote on every issue)
- the second is not something that facts alone can impose.

You may point out something to be the course of action that, in your opinion, is in my best interest, but as a free individual, I should be able to decide whether I want to accept or reject your advice. To do other than that, if I have good reasons for rejecting it, is to render self-contradictory the notion that it is in fact my 'best interest' – it cannot be 'best' for me unless it follows what I freely choose.

But how are people to decide on what legislation to agree on?

> Will it be by common agreement, or by sudden inspiration? Has the body politic an organ for expressing its will? ... How would a blind multitude, which often knows not what it wishes because it rarely knows what is good for it, execute of itself an enterprise so great, so difficult as a system of legislation?
>
> *The Social Contract*, Chapter 6 (trans. H. J. Tozer)

His answer is that a superior intelligence, in the form of a wise legislator, is needed to perform that task. Such a role is so exalted that Rousseau sees such a person as believing himself capable of changing human nature and 'substituting a social and moral existence for the independent and physical existence which we have all received from nature'. The problem is that, for its own good, the people will need to be changed for the better. That goal, for the best of reasons, has been the inspiration of many a dictator.

Rousseau mocked the British for being free only when they held an election, between which times they were content to submit to the rule of their government. That may be a valid criticism of any representative democracy, but is it any worse than continually being told that the government knows what you really want and then forcing you to have it?

Fluoride and families

Should fluoride be added to our drinking water? After all, it would improve the state of our teeth and would therefore be in the interests of all. Rousseau would not hesitate. And what else might be considered the General Will argument? Should the Chinese be 'free' to have only one child, in order to limit population growth?

Still relevant?

To some, the discussions of the seventeenth and eighteenth centuries may seem of historical interest only, but is that necessarily so? John Rawls, who is credited with doing more than anyone else in raising the interest in political philosophy over the last 30 years, presented in his *A Theory of Justice*, a thought experiment that involved people agreeing together on the basis for the redistribution of wealth within their society. We shall look at this important book later (page 91) but for now we should notice that the task of trying to justify the basis for politics may still depend on some form of contractualism, and therefore look back to the earlier Social Contract.

All modern ideas about respect for the individual, equality of opportunity, or the independence of the judiciary, for example, assume that government is done by consent, and in a way that satisfies the majority of citizens. Liberal democracy – now seen by many as the only viable political ideology – finds its origins in seventeenth-century debates. Hence, to appreciate the present, it is important not to forget the discussions of the past.

Focus groups and spin

Are the British really only free when they hold a general election, as Rousseau suggested? Today, governments may use focus groups and polls as a means of gathering information about what the public wants. But exactly how that information is used and presented, and how it is taken to justify political action, is more subtle. Facts, once used in political debate, tend to acquire a certain 'spin' – and newspapers add another spin of their own.

- Do governments tell people what they want to hear, or do they tell people, based on poll evidence, what they think people want to hear?

> • How do you balance the rights of the individual with the need for decisive action on the part of government? That is a question as relevant now as in the eighteenth century.

Of course, there is always going to be a fundamental problem with any contractual approach to establishing the authority of the state: even if it works well as a 'thought experiment', it does not represent the *actual situation*. David Hume commented (in *Of the Original Contract* 1741) that:

> Almost all governments which exist at present, or of which there remains any record in story, have been founded originally, either on usurpation or conquest, or both, without any pretence of a fair consent or voluntary subjection of the people.

He is not saying that contractual consent is wrong as a basis for government, but simply that it is not the *actual* basis for government. Most people, he argued, do not think that they have given consent to the government; they have simply been born into that country and its authority. People are not free to leave their country – especially if they are poor and know no foreign language – and they therefore have no choice but to accept the government that they are given.

Hence, any agreement between government and people is, for all practical purposes, imposed on the vast majority of citizens by accident of birth. That, of course, does not prevent them from subsequently criticizing their government – which is the provision made by Locke and enshrined in representative democracy – but it does show the very artificial nature of claiming a contract as the basis for their obedience.

Created or discovered

Finally, notice the huge shift that has taken place as we moved from the Ancient Greek and mediaeval world to the seventeenth century. In the earlier political thinking, the task was to align the operations of society with a sense of ultimate purpose, so that people could live the 'good life' and flourish. It did not depend on what individuals thought might be to their benefit, but upon a serious consideration of the purpose of life. An ideal form of government was out there to be discovered.

Now, with the theories of social contract, the emphasis has shifted to what people *want*. Whether it is the basics of democracy, the negotiations of the prisoners' dilemma or utilitarianism, it is the wishes and preferences of people that count. Government is to be constructed and shaped to fit our wishes.

The problem, from the standpoint of the individual citizen, was how – once you have created your Leviathan, or your General Will – you retain some sort of control over that political beast. How do you then avoid the possibility that you, as an individual, will not have your freedom curtailed for the supposed benefit of the whole? Here it is Locke, rather than Hobbes or Rousseau, who provides the effective possibility of political reform: the people are in charge, and they can change a government that does not satisfy their intentions.

But it leaves open a fundamental question: *Are the wishes of individual people a wise and secure basis on which to establish government and law.*

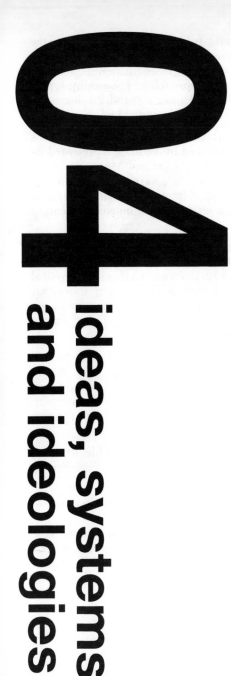

04

ideas, systems and ideologies

In this chapter you will learn:
- the difference between political philosophy and ideology
- the principles upon which political ideologies are based
- what the major political ideologies claim.

We have already seen that, from Ancient Greece to the mediaeval world, political ideas were linked to an overall view of the 'good life' and how it might be achieved. We also considered the 'social contract' approach to philosophy, which developed alongside the rise of democracy and the increased awareness of the value and rights of the individual.

By the second half of the nineteenth century, these two streams of political thought had been joined by another, represented by the work of thinkers such as Kant, Hegel and Marx. It was the era in which people were becoming aware of evolution and change. This was true, of course, in terms of Darwin and natural selection, but it was equally a feature of the nineteenth-century awareness of social change.

Hegel (1770–1831) is the philosopher who is key to this approach. He argued that reality was always embodied in the historical process, and that a nation was, in effect, the physical expression of the moral law, having a life over and above that of the individuals who comprise it. In other words, he considered that it was possible to see social and political change as part of an overall rational *system*.

That system saw history unfolding in a process of *dialectical* change, one state of affairs (a 'thesis') develops from within itself its own opposition (an 'antithesis), and these two are then resolved (in a 'synthesis'), a process which repeats over and over. For Hegel, this process expressed the *Geist*, or spirit of the age, which gave meaning to people's lives.

So political philosophy blended views of the good life, issues of contract and also these broad systems of thought developed by Hegel and later by Marx.

These form the broad base of ideas, concepts and systems of thought that are the subject matter of political philosophy. But when it comes to popular political debate, people seldom have time to go back and explain their ideas with reference to first principles, or get involved in ideas about some overall explanatory system such as Hegel and Marx expounded. Instead, they tend to opt for a pre-packaged political ideology.

What is a political ideology?

A political ideology is a set of ideas, values and arguments that hang together to give a coherent overall view of what society should be like. By the twentieth century there was a wide range of competing political ideologies on offer: socialism, communism, conservatism, liberalism, nationalism, fascism, anarchism and – more recently – environmentalism.

One danger with ideologies is that they are too convenient. They offer a way of gathering together ideas into a simplified package which can easily be used as a label or badge, and people tend to cling to them passionately and not always rationally. In reality, each of them embraces a wide range of views and ideas.

The outline of these different ideologies is a matter for politics, rather than political philosophy, but we need to be aware of them, partly because they are used in political debate, but also because they tend to be based on one or more key ideas and values:

- freedom and democracy
- established traditions and values
- justice and equality
- personal and national development
- respect for the environment.

These basic ideas may conflict with one another: freedom for one might lead to injustice for another; absolute equality might stifle personal development. So ideologies tend to take one of these as *foundational*, and will, if necessary, compromise on the others. For example, if you take freedom as your foundational value, you may need to allow inequalities in society if everyone is free to work to improve their situation, and you will probably want to limit what a government can do to curtail freedom, even if it is done in the name of justice or equality. On the other hand, if equality is seen as foundational, people's personal freedoms and ambitions may need to be restricted if they go against the needs of society as a whole.

We shall therefore take a brief look at the major political ideologies, but first a note about the generally accepted way of labelling ideas and ideologies...

Right, left or centre

The terms 'right', 'left' and 'centre' are regularly used in political discussions. They are not new, but go back to the eighteenth century.

- In general, the 'left' refers to ideologies that favour social equality and what they regard as a progressive agenda for society. Various socialist and Marxist ideologies would come under that category, as indeed would anarchists.

- By contrast, the 'right' embraces those ideologies that are more conservative by nature, favouring only gradual change and mindful of established tradition. It is also used for those ideologies, such as fascism, that accept an authoritarian and often nationalistic approach.

- The 'centre' is generally used for the liberal ideology, but it may also refer to those of either right or left who are of a moderate disposition and favour broad consensus. Hence the term 'centre-right' may be used for moderate conservatives, and social democrats may refer to themselves as occupying the 'centre-left' of the political spectrum.

Starting with freedom and democracy

If freedom is taken as the foundational value, then a society will seek to allow individuals to maximize their life opportunities without hindrance from government. Legislation will be kept to a minimum, sufficient to protect people from harming one another, but otherwise, society should tolerate in an individual or group whatever does not interfere with the freedom of others.

At one extreme, you have **libertarianism**. This argues for complete freedom for the individual, and sees the state as exercising minimal control. But this position raises some questions:

- What are the consequences of allowing everyone to do exactly what they want?
- People need to work together in society, is that compatible with complete freedom?
- Can I be free to take drugs, refuse to pay taxes, have sex with children, without these things impacting on the lives and welfare of others?

- Does a non-interventionist view of government benefit only the articulate better-off who stand most chance of doing what they like?
- Does government have any role (as Plato and Aristotle argued) in shaping and guiding the life of individuals, rather than just responding to their wishes?

Such questions about freedom (to which we shall return in Chapter 06) tend to suggest that we should take a more moderate position – **liberalism.**

Liberalism, as we know it today, developed in the seventeenth and eighteenth centuries. It was an ideology based on respect for the individual, and sought to enable the individual to retain control of his or her life to the maximum extent possible, to be limited only by the necessity to ensure that this same liberty was available to all other people as well – a view clearly set out in the nineteenth century by John Stuart Mill.

Liberalism is often associated with individualism – the claim that individuals should be free to make their own choices and that the state should provide an environment in which such individual choices can be made and put into effect.

However, this liberal quest for freedom took several different (and to some extent, conflicting) directions. If I wish to be free, it is reasonable that I should want to be free economically as well as politically. I may want to start a business and will want to do so with the minimum of state interference or regulation. This has led to what is sometimes referred to as **neo-liberalism** which is the view that there should be a largely de-regularized, low-tax economy.

Curiously, neo-liberalism may be seen as part of the 'new-right' – and thus have roots as much in conservatism (see page 64) as traditional liberalism. Freedom of trade is not simply the freedom of the individual, it is the freedom to develop and increase the value of one's business, and that can only happen in a competitive environment. Deregulation may lead to better goods and services being produced, as each provider is required to compete against all others for a share of the market. The freedom to win also implies the freedom to lose, and so a deregulated economy may therefore be both threatening and challenging.

Typical of this approach was that of Margaret Thatcher when Prime Minister of Great Britain. By cutting regulation and taxes and selling off state businesses and council houses, it was argued that people would be encouraged to take responsibility for themselves, and keep more of their own money to do with as they wished, buying health care and education from the private sector if they so chose. Although notionally 'conservative' this approach was clearly what we would call 'neo-liberal'.

The great libertarian economist Adam Smith (1723–90) argued that the state should not interfere with the private interests of individuals or with the working of the free-market. Once freed from political control, capitalist free-markets spring up naturally (as argued, for example, by the modern economist Milton Friedman). Hence, the neo-liberal tradition, in removing political control to limit the economic freedom of individuals, encourages economics to take on a life of its own in shaping society.

Adam Smith did not deny that a capitalist system delivered inequality of wealth. His point, however, was that the *overall* wealth of a nation would increase. In other words, even if the rich became proportionately richer, what they generated would also improve the situation of the poorest.

The economy first

In some political discussions it is assumed that the prime aim of government is to encourage an increase in the standard of living of its people and therefore an increase in the choice of goods and services on offer. Delivering economic success seems to be the first responsibility of government, once internal and external security is taken care of.

- Is it universally agreed that economic development is the main goal in life?
- If other factors – the quality of the environment, for example – were given priority, what implications might that have?

The other development of liberal thought, and one which develops directly out of its original respect for the autonomy of the individual, is that of civil and human rights. If a person is to be respected, then their rights must be defended. Yet the defence of human rights may well require legislation and restraint of those who would exploit others. Hence the same liberal value of respect for the individual may find itself on very different sides of the debate about economic freedom. Giving people complete economic freedom may well leave open the possibility of inequality and exploitation. Regulating them in favour of the basic rights of the individual, may be seen as the frustration of a natural form of self-expression and development.

The dilemma for a liberal is how to protect and encourage individuals at one and the same time – how to prevent them from harming themselves, while granting them the freedom to do so if they wish.

Participation

Thinkers such as Hannah Arendt (1906–75) argued that there is little scope in modern liberal democracy for participation in the political process. She looks to a more **republican** level of participation – in other words, like the republics of Ancient Greece and the Italian Renaissance – in which a significant number of people are directly involved with political decision-making on behalf of the people as a whole. This links to the idea of the 'public sphere' (a term introduced by Jürgen Habermas, b. 1929, a German social thinker and philosopher). Everyone has two spheres of operation in their lives, one public and the other private. For Arendt and Habermas, the public one should be given greater prominence. The danger of modern liberal society is that the individual is considered as interested only in their 'private sphere' as a consumer of goods and services for themselves and their family, whereas political engagement is a matter of getting involved with the whole public arena of political debate and action.

Habermas's ideal of the public sphere is in stark contrast to what is often found in democracies today – namely that decision-making is limited to a minority of enthusiasts or professionals, working within political parties. The bulk of citizens may or may not opt to vote in a general election, but otherwise see themselves as no more than passive recipients of a political system into which they have no effective input. The ideal of republicanism, and of the 'public space' which is its modern articulation, is one of participation, of each person being able to engage in the political process at an appropriate level.

Anarchism

Pushed to its logical extreme, the quest for freedom leads to **anarchism**. This is the view that government is at best unnecessary and at worst harmful. It has a long history and is associated with very different thinkers. Of those already mentioned in this book, Diogenes the Cynic certainly resented any type of rule or the requirement that one should conform to the expectations of society, and Rousseau felt that the natural state of humankind was corrupted by society.

Anarchism as an ideology developed in the nineteenth century and is particularly associated with the work of William Godwin (1756–1836), Pierre-Joseph Proudhon (1809–65) and Peter Kropotkin (1842–1921). As you might expect, anarchists were not well organized with a single, centrally-agreed political agenda! There are many different forms of anarchism, some emphasizing freedom of the individual, others the value of collective action, but all seem to hold the basic view that humankind can flourish naturally and spontaneously once political constraints are removed. Anarchism therefore holds a *positive* view of human nature and potential, but a generally *cynical* view of the value of political structures.

Starting with established values and traditions

For some, established values and traditions are not to be set aside lightly, especially if they are seen to be effective in regulating society. **Conservatism** is less an ideology and more a general attitude towards society and politics. It sees value in the established traditions of society, promotes law and order, seeks to cherish what has been achieved in the past, and encourages respect for authority. If there is to be change, it should be cautious, based on experience rather than abstract thinking.

The classic text expressing the heart of conservatism is Edmund Burke's *Reflexions on the Revolution in France*, published in 1792. Burke (1729–97) appeals for a slow process of change in society, one which recognizes the cumulative wisdom of the past. He, of course, was in favour of a constitutional monarchy, set alongside the democratic institutions of government, as had been established in England. To understand the force of Burke's argument one has only to read his implacable opponent,

Thomas Paine. His *Rights of Man* is written to counter Burke's argument at every step. Looking at the battle between their positions you see the fundamental division between conservative and socialist thinking – with Paine pushing for the overthrow of all restraining authority and a deep trust in the ability of people to agree together, and Burke constantly arguing caution and trust in the establishment.

Modern conservatism has been modified to fit the spirit of the age and has taken on the key features of liberalism. Indeed, the neo-conservative agenda in terms of the economy is very much one of liberal *laissez-faire*. Hence, you have Margaret Thatcher's 'liberal' economic reforms, presented from a conservative point of view, and aimed at rolling back the amount of state interference in people's lives. Under John Major, the Conservative party argued for the theme of 'back to basics', and it has tended to be the party of law and order, lower taxation, respect for authority and the defence of private property, along with a sense of duty and national pride.

Neo-conservatism, a particular phenomenon of political thinking in the United States in recent years, is rather different from conventional conservatism, and more heavily dependent on the liberal economic agenda. As outlined by Fukuyama (in *America at the Crossroads,* 2006) it has four distinguishing features:

- that the internal character and the values embodied in a political regime are important, and should be expressed in its foreign policy. (Particularly in shaping the foreign policy of the USA to reflect its liberal democratic values.)
- the belief that America should remain engaged in foreign affairs and should use its power for moral purposes
- a sceptical view of the value of social planning
- a sceptical view of the ability of international law or international institutions to be effective in securing security and justices.

In particular, as described by Fukuyama, the neo-conservatives considered that it was right for the United States to use its military power to achieve a 'benevolent hegemony' of those parts of the world that it considered to be of strategic importance.

We will consider the neo-conservative position again, in connection with the role of the state, and the response to war and terrorism. For now, however, it is important to note that the conservative and neo-conservative positions tend to emphasize what they see as a moral responsibility to maintain traditional values. Exactly how traditional those values are, or how they may be justified rationally, is of course another matter.

Mill's criticism of following custom

'The despotism of custom is everywhere the standing hindrance to human advancement, being in unceasing antagonism to that disposition to aim at something better than customary, which is called, according to circumstances, the spirit of liberty, or that of progress or improvement.'

John Stuart Mill, *On Liberty* (1863)

- But notice that neo-conservatism stands closer to libertarianism or liberalism than the old-style, custom-based conservatism against which Mill is arguing here. Neo-conservatism pushes a libertarian economic agenda.

Starting with equality

If you take fairness and equality as your foundational value, you are going to be concerned that everyone in society receives what they need, and that a privileged minority does not control a nation's economic base in order to benefit at the expense of others.

To some extent this is already being considered in Plato and Aristotle (although with huge reservations, since women and slaves were largely ignored or patronized in their thinking), and it is reflected in 'social contract' thinking, by emphasizing the responsibility of the people for their own destiny, rather than being under the control of an unaccountable or autocratic ruler.

But with the nineteenth century – with huge changes to society with the industrial revolution, the development of capitalism and the formation of an urban, industrial working class – this thinking developed into the **socialist** and **communist** ideologies.

Socialism sprang out of a practical concern for the working class and a revolt against the social impact of unfettered capitalism. It argued that capitalism needed to be tempered by political or social aims. Slave labour and child labour are now illegal, not for capitalist reasons, but for *social* ones – even if profitable, they should not be allowed. Philosophers such as Bertrand Russell (in his lecture 'The Case for Socialism') have argued against a general tendency, inherent in capitalism, to encourage inequality, to ignore the plight of those who are unemployed, and to allow the development of an underclass. It presented itself as something of a moral crusade against the fundamentals of capitalism – which led to alienation, exploitation and treating people as commodities and as cogs in an economic wheel.

Robert Owen (1771–1858), an early socialist, argued (in *A New View of Society*, 1814) that small groups of people, responsible for their own work, could band together and rule themselves in a co-operative fashion. He believed that people were influenced by their environment, and so set about forming a community for mill workers (he himself having worked as a manager and owner of cotton mills in New Lanark, Scotland). He saw his reforms as something of a moral crusade, improving the conditions of working people. Interestingly, when in 1813 he sought funds from people who were prepared to invest in his milling business for a more modest return (five per cent) in order to give him scope for his social reforms, one of those to do so was the utilitarian Jeremy Bentham.

In some ways, such socialism was not so far removed from early anarchists, who argued that people could work together quite well without the imposition of political control on behalf of the state – but they did so in the very different circumstances of the newly industrialized working class. Self-government through reason, getting beyond the old established divisions of the past (including the divisions brought about by religion) were his theme.

Broadly, a socialist ideology seeks to redistribute wealth in favour of the least well-off, to restrain those aspects of capitalism that might produce socially unacceptable consequences. Socialists wanted the production of goods to be locked into an overall framework for society, and not simply be left to free-market capitalist economics. Hence the development of trade unionism – as representing the interests of working people, and aiming to improve the terms and conditions.

Therefore the fundamental distinction between a capitalist and a socialist society is about whether the needs of capital dominate over those of society, or vice versa. In practice, of course, almost all states will fall in between those two extremes – the main thing is to sort out where the balance point comes.

Permission needed?

Having quoted Mill's criticism of a conservative approach, it is only fair to note that, in *On Liberty*, he is equally critical of a society where the State organizes everything – a tendency of socialist states. In context, however, Mill was actually arguing against the dominance of bureaucracy, which he saw exemplified by Russia under the rule of the Czar.

> 'In countries of more advanced civilization and of a more insurrectionary spirit, the public, accustomed to expect everything to be done for them by the State, or at least to do nothing for themselves without asking from the State not only leave to do it, but even how it is to be done, naturally hold the State responsible for all evil which befalls them, and when the evil exceeds their amount of patience, they rise against the government and make what is called a revolution; whereupon somebody else, with or without legitimate authority from the nation, vaults into the seat, issues his order to the bureaucracy, and everything goes on much as it did before; the bureaucracy being unchanged, and nobody else being capable of taking their place.'

- All too often 'they ought to do something about it' is an excuse for political inactivity!

Marx and communism

Karl Marx (1818–83) famously said 'Philosophers have only interpreted the world in various ways, the real point is to change it' and, without doubt, his own political philosophy has been hugely influential, and shaped much of the history of the twentieth century. His principal work was *Das Kapital*, published in 1867. The literature on Marx is vast, and it is unrealistic to try to summarize his work in this short section, but it is important to 'place' him within the overall development of political philosophy.

Marx argued that political and social structures were fundamentally rooted in economics, and specifically in the production and distribution of goods. He therefore interpreted history in economic terms and as shaped by the struggle between the social classes: with capitalist employers facing their employees as once landowners faced their peasants.

Everything is seen in terms of the class struggle, and in the context of society as a whole.

Marx was influenced by Hegel's 'dialectic' (see page 58) but considered that it was driven by the material and economic basis of society. Hence, his theory is called **dialectical materialism**.

Marx thought that, in a capitalist system, wage labourers, producing something from which someone else makes a profit, become alienated from their work, and are treated as impersonal 'things' – machines whose sole purpose in life is production. He saw the capitalist process leading to more and more wealth being concentrated in the hands of a small number of 'bourgeoisie', with the working 'proletariat' declining into poverty. He argued that this would eventually lead those workers to rise up against the bourgeois owners of property, gain common ownership of the means of production, and establish a classless society – the dictatorship of the proletariat: communism.

Communist ideology generally involves a high degree of state control, since private enterprise and capitalism were a feature of the failing, earlier regime. It also entailed the provision of the essentials of life in the form of a welfare state.

Within the ideology there have been significant differences of emphasis. Under Lenin, the state gained power, whereas Trotsky wanted less formal power to be in the hands of the communist party machine, and more direct involvement of people in political decision-making. Mao, in China, was faced with a different situation from that envisaged by Marx, and saw the ordinary working people in the agricultural environment as ready to lead a revolution, as opposed to Marx's assumption that the agricultural world would need to give way to an industrialized one before such a revolution could happen.

However, under communism, the apparatus of the state, far from withering away, which was Marx's original prediction, grew and became increasingly directive in terms of every aspect of human life, defensive of their ideology. Political debate was discouraged, and those with dissenting ideas brutally repressed.

The other key factor in assessing Marxist ideology was that it predicted the eventual self-destruction of capitalism, and the flourishing of a classless, communist society. In practice, of course, capitalism has flourished into the twenty-first century, and Marxist states have failed to deliver the equality and freedom promised, and have therefore either failed or been overthrown, compromised with the capitalist system, or retreated behind strict ideological borders.

For Soviet Communism, a terrible dilemma emerged in 1956, when the truth about Stalin's rule of terror was finally acknowledged and denounced by Khrushchev at the twentieth Congress of the Communist Party. It is sometimes referred to as 'the Great Contradiction' and can be expressed thus:

- Was Stalin's rule the inevitable product of economic structures that created it?
- Or was it the cult of personality that allowed Stalin to rule in that way, shaping society and standing above the law?

If you take the first of these options, then the inevitable march of dialectical materialism led to a disaster, not the ideal society and the rule of the proletariat, and Marx had argued that a society would produce the leaders it needed. Hence the Soviet system itself could be blamed for producing Stalin.

But if you take the second of these options, it means that dialectical materialism itself is fundamentally wrong, and that change happens through the influence of individual rulers, not the outworking of the dialectic.

Faced with the reality of what had happened in the Soviet Union under Stalin, it suddenly seemed that Marx's most basic view of the nature of political change was either fundamentally flawed, or its results utterly unacceptable. It was a traumatic acknowledgement from which Communism never really recovered.

Friedrich von Hayek (1899–1992), in his book *The Road to Serfdom* (1944) criticized all ideologies based on collectivism – namely the idea that economic activity should be organized centrally by the state – on the grounds that collectivism led naturally to totalitarianism. He believed that central planning would never achieve fairness in the distribution of resources, which was best left to market forces, and the ability of people to get together spontaneously and co-operate for mutual benefit. In practice, the huge centralized economy of the Soviet Union under Stalin, for example, was seen to be hopelessly inefficient, bogged down in bureaucracy, and maintained by totalitarian ruthlessness.

Another major criticism of Marxist communism came from Karl Popper (1902–94). Marx saw progress of society as scientifically determined by dialectical materialism, but Popper argued that this was bogus science, since Marxists would not allow anything to refute their theory, and that it led to a fixed and totalitarian view of the future. This was in line with his main contribution to the philosophy of science – falsification – namely that in order to test a theory, one needs to know what would show it to be false, since no genuine theory is compatible with contradictory pieces of evidence. Marxists would allow nothing to count against the truth of dialectical materialism, therefore, he argued, the theory could not be genuinely scientific. This undermined the foundations of communist social theory.

Consumers and the means of production

Socialism traditionally considered the collectivization of the means of production as a necessary step on the way to its political goal. Once the state has direct control of the means of production, there could be a radical shift – namely that the economy could be run for the sake of satisfying the genuine needs of the people – whereas under capitalism, ever-increasing needs are stimulated in people in order to feed the needs of a self-perpetuating capitalist system.

Chicken and egg on phones

Are new mobile phone models produced in order to meet the needs of those who will use them? Or are new possible uses devised in order to sell more mobile phones?

Of these two options, the second seems the more likely, given the way in which the market is stimulated within a capitalist system. Yet, from the point of view of those who enjoy the newly-devised benefits, does that really matter? If the end result is that everyone has a more interesting or attractive piece of equipment, does it matter whether its production was the result of philanthropic idealism, or the desire for enhanced profits?

The overall success of capitalism and the failure of planned economies has meant that – broadly speaking – the socialist position today is not one that would try to eliminate the capitalist system, or the general principles of supply and demand that are built into it. Rather, it suggests that capitalism should be gently regulated, recognizing that naked competition (as presented by Plato's Thasymachus, where justice is whatever is in the interests of the stronger) does not always give an acceptable social outcome.

Modern social democracy is the result of this fusion of socialism with a recognition of the benefits to working people that can be brought by an economy that delivers ever-increasing standards of living. And that recognition has moved modern socialist parties a considerable distance towards the liberal agenda.

Left *v.* right on housing?

Until the 1980s, Britain had a growing (though never adequate) stock of council houses for rent. People who could not afford to buy their own homes had a reasonable prospect of renting, albeit after waiting their turn for the next property to become vacant. Then in the 1980s the then Prime Minister, Margaret Thatcher, advanced the policy of selling off council houses to their tenants, thereby claiming to set them free into the world of property ownership.

That housing stock was not replaced, and even in the first decade of the twenty-first century relatively few new and affordable homes are available for rent, at the very time when inflation has taken the cost of home ownership beyond the means of many young working people. Former council houses have sometimes changed hands many times. Having originally been sold to their tenants at a discount, they may now come on the market at a price beyond the reach of those who three decades ago would have been able to rent them.

Here is a clear example of the old left/right divide on policy:

- The old socialist policy was to provide affordable housing.
- The liberal/conservative policy was to give people the flexibility of home ownership, releasing the energy locked up in the inertia of renting a drab property for which one did not have responsibility.

Today, all sides admit that there is a serious need for more affordable housing, but the last decade of rule by New Labour has not seen a return to the former policy of massive house building by local councils. The old left/right divide on housing has become blurred, with little desire to return to the old policy of building massive new council estates, but much hand wringing about the problems of young people taking on mortgages that they stand little chance of being able to repay.

Socialism and the work-based economy

André Gorz was a major European contributor to thinking about socialism and capitalism, who was also concerned with political ecology – relating political decisions to lifestyle and environment. In *Capitalism, Socialism and Ecology* (1991) he criticized 'the domination of the economic rationality embodied in capitalism.' In other words, from a socialist point of view, he was concerned not just about the social impact of economics, but about what he saw as the domination of political thinking by economics.

A critique of the supply and demand economy

If the price of agricultural produce or the level of wages were determined by the laws of supply and demand, most of us would have died of starvation long ago. In all industrialized nations, the relative price of goods and services are regulated by the state; if they weren't society wouldn't be viable. ... The fact is that the market is, by definition, the outcome of the activities of individuals each pursuing his or her immediate interests. Thus a higher authority, the state, is required to take responsibility for defending the general interest, including the existence of a market system.

André Gorz, *Capitalism, Socialism and Ecology*
(pp. 82–3)

Work and workers had changed – from a solid body of working-class full-time labourers, to part-time jobs in the service sectors, largely taken by women, and those whose jobs were on short-term contracts or were otherwise precarious. Gorz referred to those in such work, along with the unemployed, as the 'post-industrial proletariat'. The situation is also changing because work may now no longer be the key feature of people's lives – people want to work fewer hours in order to pursue other cultural or social activities.

Gorz argued that it is no longer necessary for wages to be paid in relation to the number of hours worked, because some processes require less labour than they did before, and that tradition of paying for hours worked is continued simply in order to maintain domination over the new post-industrial proletariat. He believes that the new proletariat should be guaranteed the right to a sufficient basic income so that they do not have to be anxious about the temporary and fragile security brought by work.

If society no longer needs the number of workers or man-hours it once did, then there should be some other way of allowing all to have an income, and to share out such work as is available. The capitalist system, by contrast, makes the struggle for work competitive, and thereby forces its value down, enabling companies to make greater profits. Gorz is therefore looking for a society where fairness does not depend on the work contribution, but without taking away the competitiveness or efficiency of companies (since he acknowledges that there is no alternative economic theory to capitalism – he's not going back to the old planned economy). He argues for a guaranteed wage, funded by indirect taxation, which would therefore have no effect on the balance of competitiveness between companies.

In other words, even if capitalism is the driving force in a competitive market, the priority for a socialist like Gorz was to find a way in which everyone is guaranteed a fair share of resources, irrespective of what he or she can contribute in terms of marketable skills.

Postscript to Gorz

As this book was being written, news came of the death of André Gorz. President Nicolas Sarkozy described him as 'a major intellectual figure of the French and European left who spent all his life in a profound analysis of both socialism and capitalism.' In 2006, aged 83, he wrote an open letter to his wife of 58 years, Dorine, giving the story of their love. She was terminally ill, and he could not bear the thought of attending her funeral. On 22 September 2007, having written letters explaining their action to friends and officials, and leaving instructions for their funeral, they ended their lives together.

Starting with personal or national development

In a world that is changing and developing, it is important for both individuals and nations to set goals and aspire to achieve them, and these can become the key feature of a social, political or personal ideology.

Friedrich Nietzsche (1844–1900) is a most fascinating and challenging philosopher, best known for his claim that God is dead and that humankind must therefore take responsibility for its own future. At a time when Darwin's theory of natural selection, and the idea of evolution generally, was bringing new perspectives to an understanding of the human species, Nietzsche boldly saw man as poised on a tightrope moving from beast towards a higher future form: his *übermensch* or 'superman'.

He declares his *übermensch* to be the meaning of the earth and in a key passage in *Thus Spoke Zarathustra* says:

> All creatures hitherto have created something beyond themselves: and do you want to be the ebb of this great tide, and return to the animals rather than overcoming man?
>
> (Translated by Hollingdale, Penguin)

His affirmation of life is expressed as a 'will to power' – not the crude power of Plato's Thasymachus, but a will to affirm life, to develop and move forward. In this he criticizes both Christianity and democracy, since he believes that they hold back the strong for the sake of the weak. Indeed, Christianity appears to him to celebrate weakness and to willingly accept a 'slave morality' of protection, rather than a 'master morality' of self-development and the cultivation of the noble virtues.

Nietzsche is heady stuff, but well worth reading. For our purposes we need only touch on some political implications of his work – namely, that evolution and personal development, both for the individual and for society, can be taken as a *foundational* value. In other words, producing the *übermensch* is the *starting point* – the necessary function by which society, and therefore a political system, is to be judged.

Sadly, Nietzsche was read by both Hitler and Mussolini, and a caricature of his work was taken as justification for their

militant nationalism and, under the Nazis, to the most extreme
form of racism, with brutal results.

Nationalism is not a political ideology, but is an expression of
political power, related to the nation state. It is compatible with
other ideologies, but sets over them the priority of the
development of the nation state, giving added weight to
patriotism, and often emphasizing the importance of the nation
as opposed to international or religious organizations.

At the extreme right, nationalist sympathies move towards
fascism. Here the national identity is used as a backing for the
introduction of a totalitarian regime, with opposition to liberal
ideas, and a radical requirement for individuals to conform to the
national or cultural stereotype. Mussolini in Italy, Hitler in
Germany and Franco in Spain are examples of this approach – in
each case there seems to have been a considerable cult of the leader,
in which the ruler is seen as the embodiment of national ideals.

But fascism is not without its philosophical backing. Hegel had
argued that individuals find in the state the expression of their
collective will and consciousness. They therefore seek an ideal
state and an ideal leader, gathering and giving focus to their
collective aspirations. An early exponent of this fascist ideology
was the neo-Hegelian philosopher Giovanni Gentile
(1875–1944), whose theory of Actual Idealism was intended to
overcome the gap between ideas and action, so that people
expressed their philosophy through political commitment. Similar
sentiments are also to be found in Heidegger, who supported the
Nazi Party on the grounds that people, thrown into a particular
place in life by the accident of their birth, needed a sense of
direction, and that could only be given by a strong leader.

To change the world ...

Gentile has the dubious distinction of being philosophy's only
political ghost writer, having written Mussolini's *The Doctrine of
Fascism*, but his ideas stand in interesting contrast to those of
Marx. Where Marx took Hegel's dialectic and based it in the
material, economic world, Gentile retained a dialectic of ideas.
Both believed that their philosophy would change society; both
were idealists. Whether their value as philosophers should be
completely tarnished by the political structures that grew from
their ideas is another matter.

When Machiavelli considered what was required to hold power in a city-state in Renaissance Italy, he saw clearly that ruthlessness was sometimes more effective than indecisive kindness. The priority for a ruler, in his view, was the security, integrity and strength of the state – that was his foundational value, and all that he allows by way of freedom or equality must take second place to establishing it.

So the key question here is:

• To what extend should the development of the state, in terms of its strength, security, stability and economic viability take precedence over the values of freedom and equality for its people?

Dictators

The key feature of dictators is that they stand above the rule of law and the political process. They reflect many different ideologies, from the extreme left to the extreme right, but share a ruthless determination to organize and control the nations they lead. Some, like Stalin, cause the death of millions.

The head of a military coup may become a dictator, simply because of the rigid chain of command and the absolute nature of military discipline, preventing a challenge to established authority – as in the case of present-day Burma. However, a dictatorship may sometimes be justified in terms of its ability to control an otherwise unruly situation by force; Saddam ruled Iraq and held the country together only by the brutal suppression of opposition. It is relevant to ask whether anything less than a dictatorship is capable of holding together a state with such opposing internal factions. On that question, only time will tell.

Historically, dictators have generally come to power in situations which required decisive political action, and have sometimes been welcomed by the people for the benefits that decisiveness can offer in terms of the efficiency of the services provided by the government. The problem is that, once in power, it is difficult to remove them, since they control the military and other means of effecting change.

The pro-democracy demonstrations in Burma have so far failed to remove the military rule of General Than Shwe, simply because the generals have the power to repress the demonstrations. That is the nature of military dictatorships.

In other states, military rule may be imposed on the grounds of national security and the need for decisive action, with the intention of handing over power to a democratically elected government once that is achieved – an example of this might be President Musharraf of Pakistan. Although, at the time of writing, with a state of emergency declared and the main opposition leaders under house arrest, it remains to be seen whether democracy will be reinstated. In the face of internal and external pressure, there is a tendency for dictators, in the name of the integrity and security of the state, to prefer the status quo to the democratic process.

Starting with the environment

With 6.5 billion people on this planet, limited natural resources, and a global economy that encourages increased consumption of goods and services, it is not surprising that the human impact on the environment is growing, and the recognition of this has led to the development of a set of ethical and political guidelines that challenge existing ideologies.

Capitalism and the environment

'An economic system that requires constant growth, while bucking almost all serious attempts at environmental regulation, generates a steady stream of disasters all on its own, whether military, ecological or financial.'

Quoted from Naomi Klein's book *The Shock Doctrine: The Rise of Disaster Capitalism*, Allen Lance, 2007, which offers a critique of neo-liberalism.

To some, mention of the environment suggests that the operation of industry, transport and so on should take into account the environmental impact. This may be fine in itself, but it does not address the fundamental assumption of capitalism that there will be an ever-increasing number of goods and services, produced to meet stimulated needs. To some (for example André Gorz) this seems to be no more than a partial response to the global environmental crisis, since it leaves the structure of production that causes environmental damage in place.

The alternative is a more radical ecological approach which steps back from the economic assumptions of capitalism and asks why we need to increase our standard of living (which is usually taken to be identical with our levels of consumption). This approach would suggest that quality of life may be improved by consuming less rather than more – approaching life and its values from the ecological perspective, and then refining our perceived needs and desires in the light of that perspective rather than simply pressing on with the assumption of increased production.

Scramble for the seabed

John Locke argued that you acquired property by mixing your labour with the resources provided by nature – ploughing up virgin land is, in effect, to stake your claim on it. But should there be limits to the legalized appropriation of what is freely available to all? If so, how might they be set?

Under the 'UN Law of the Sea Convention', due to come into effect if a few years' time, every island, however small, will qualify for a 350-mile zone in the surrounding ocean for the exclusive exploitation of minerals and hydrocarbons. Hence small islands, like Rockall in the North Atlantic, or Ascension or the Falklands in the South, would take on new status, as potential sources of wealth for the nation that 'owns' them (in these examples, Britain) and is therefore able to extend its territorial claims. There is likely to be a scramble for nations to stake their claims before a 2009 deadline for registration.

- What right should an individual nation have to such stretches of open ocean and its resources?
- What might be the global impact of finding even more fossil fuel resources?

Political ecology is the term generally used for this re-shaping of political thought to take into account the fact that people depend on an environment that is increasingly threatened by their own activity. But there is a fundamental question to be asked:

- Should the environment be protected for its own sake, or because of its value for humankind?

Those who take the latter view point to the need for biodiversity, for example, because it is often from rare plant species that we derive new medicines. Equally, they may argue that damage to the environment will have a direct impact on the quality of life, or even the survival of the human species.

Those who take the former view (generally termed **deep ecology**) argue that we should get beyond an anthropocentric view of nature – that the environment should be protected, irrespective of whether we can see any direct benefit to humankind in doing so. This is related to the moral argument for animal rights – that other species are not there simply for entertainment or food for humans, but should be valued in themselves and treated with respect.

Clearly, political ecology involves a whole raft of issues, from climate change and pollution to the dangers of exploiting the earth's finite resources or the extinction of other species. At one time, such issues might have been regarded as primarily of moral concern to individuals, but in recent decades it has become clear that no individual, and indeed no single nation, is able to tackle these issues alone. Any fundamental change is going to require political decisions to be taken at a global as well as a national level, and the activity of individual citizens (for example, in recycling or the economical use of resources) will need some measure of political support in order to be effective.

This environmental ideology is seen in the various Green Parties within politics, as well as those organizations such as Friends of the Earth and Greenpeace that campaign on green issues. With the increasing awareness of the importance of these issues, they are also being addressed by the other political parties. Hence we have an ideology that is not simply linked to a distinctive political party, but is able to engage people from across the political spectrum, recognizing that other values cannot be maintained if the environment itself is destroyed. At whatever level it operates, the nexus of ideas and values represented by environmentalism and ecology is going to present a significant challenge to existing political and economic systems and values.

The future of ideologies

As the twentieth century came towards its end, the consensus view was that socialism, as a political theory and system, was dead. The attempt to manage national economies on ideological lines could not match what the free markets could offer by way of innovation and improvements in lifestyle. Even the traditional class structures within capitalist economies looked dated, as old class consciousness gave way to overlapping circles of allegiance in a multicultural, money-motivated, consumer-orientated environment.

Francis Fukuyama (in *The End of History and the Last Man*, 1992) argued that the global aspirations of people to share in the benefits of modern life would eventually lead them all to chose a liberal democratic form of government and a capitalist economic system. He wrote, of course, in the light of the collapse of the Soviet Union and the global retreat of socialism and communism.

Fukuyama thus saw no 'coherent *theoretical* alternatives to liberal democracy', but assumed that – like wagons moving towards a town – everyone would eventually end up in the same place, even if some had gone off the road or taken a different route, or some were making slower progress than others. In other words, that we are all headed in the same direction politically.

Fifteen years is a long time in politics, and Fukuyama has since disowned his original support of the neo-conservative agenda in the United States, in particular its foreign policy and response to the attacks of 9/11 (see page 189). It is far from clear today whether everyone who is free to choose would automatically opt for liberal-democracy and a free-market approach. As we shall see later, there are other elements in play today, in particular the rise of religious fundamentalist ideologies that cut across any simple economic assumptions. A suicide bomber is not out to increase his or her share of material benefits!

In general, the starkly contrasting ideologies that proved so lethal in the course of the twentieth century are now mellowing. The agenda has changed and new global issues pose questions to which the old ideological responses give no satisfactory answer. Liberal democracy may have won the day in terms of global influence, but as time goes on there is an increasing number of questions to be asked of its approach. It is also increasingly challenged from a religious and particularly a fundamentalist perspective as well as from the perspective of political ecology – seen particularly as the issue of global warming.

The old packages of ideas that formed the ideologies of the twentieth century are seen by some as no longer sufficiently flexible to do justice to the complex set of issues facing global, national and local communities today. Hence, rather than getting stuck with ideological labels, it is important for political philosophy to address its fundamental ideas directly, and it is to these that we must now turn.

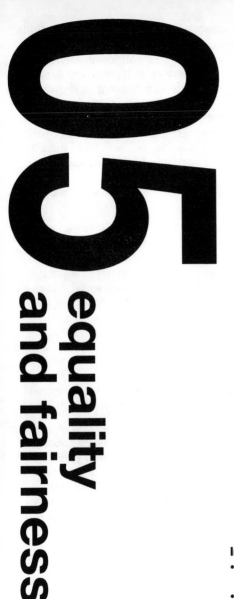

05 equality and fairness

In this chapter you will learn:
- about what constitutes a fair sharing of resources
- about the impact of the economy on political life
- about capitalism and equality
- about democracy and the problem of minorities.

The phrase 'It's the economy, stupid', first used during Bill Clinton's successful presidential campaign against George Bush in 1992, highlights the way politics and politicians are judged today. In 1992 it referred to the fact that America was in recession, and the Clinton campaign team wanted to show that as a failure of the Bush administration. Increasingly, governments are being judged on their ability to deliver on the economy, and opposition parties are concerned to set out their economic policies, in the hope that electors will trust them to run the country better than the present administration. When it comes to election time, therefore, the economy is key. But why should the economy have such importance in the assessment of political life?

Essentially, people want to feel that they are being treated fairly, for example, that they are not paying too much tax in relation to what they receive back from the government. They complain if another section of the population is being given benefits that they are denied – whether it is tax incentives or social security payments – on the grounds that people should be treated *equally* and *fairly*.

Foundational values

When thinking through any problem, it is useful to start by establishing your own *foundational values* – in other words, those things on which you are convinced and on which you are therefore unwilling to compromise.

Two key foundational values for political philosophy are *equality* and *freedom*. We have already seen that the first is generally taken as the starting point by philosophers who favour a socialist approach to politics, the second by those of a liberal persuasion. In examining issues of equality and fairness, the key question is to what extent liberty is compromised in order to secure them.

There are, of course, many other ways in which people want to be treated fairly and equally, but the sharing out of material resources is a good place to start, and to do this we need to step back and look at two key features of the political landscape: utilitarianism and capitalism.

Utilitarianism and capitalism

Utilitarianism is the ethical theory based, broadly, on the idea that the right thing to do is that which offers the prospect of the greatest benefit to the greatest number of people involved. Developed by Jeremy Bentham (1748–1832) and John Stuart Mill (1806–73), it is probably the most widely used ethical theory today. There are three main forms of utilitarianism:

- act utilitarianism assesses the results of particular actions
- rule utilitarianism adds to this a consideration of the overall benefit offered to society in maintaining general rules
- preference utilitarianism requires that everyone's preferences should be taken into account – in other words, taking note of what people see as to their benefit, rather than telling them.

The 'principle of utility' therefore required that a political system should be judged according to whether it produced more or less benefit, welfare and happiness for the greatest number of its citizens. In terms of political philosophy, utilitarianism would therefore seem to be a logical implication of democracy. If everyone can take part in electing a government, the expectation is that the government will then operate to the benefit of the majority. Indeed, that principle, although not couched in utilitarian terms, goes back to Plato and Aristotle. In a just society, it is the interests of the majority, rather than that of an elite, that should prevail.

Prison officers' pay and inflation

When Gordon Brown argued that prison officers should not be offered a pay deal that went beyond the Government's two per cent ceiling on public sector pay claims, he said:

> 'We have succeeded in tackling inflation and having a stable economy because of discipline in pay over these last ten years ... We will do nothing, nothing to put that at risk, because an absolutely essential element of maintaining discipline in the economy [is] so that people [can] have jobs and higher standards of living.'

Quoted in an article by Ben Russell, *The Independent*, 31 August 2007

- Notice here that the argument is not about the relative value of the work prison officers do, or about the inherent fairness or otherwise of their present pay. It is about the effect of individual settlements on the overall economy. It is an economic, rather than a political answer to the question of pay settlements.

- The problem here is that a settlement of 30 per cent for a company director, since it applies to a small number of individuals, will have relatively little effect on the overall economy. The more numerous the group claiming a pay rise, the more macro its economic effects.
- The implication of this is that, for the benefit of all, those groups of workers whose wages have a significant impact on the economy will need to have their aspirations overruled for the general good. Minorities who have no such impact are not required to conform in the same way.
- Here we see the impact of a utilitarian political assessment – 'the greatest good for the greatest number' – takes precedence.

Capitalism is generally regarded as the obvious way of delivering what a utilitarian assessment requires, and it is assumed that the task of government is to get out of the way and allow capitalist market forces to deliver the goods, providing the standard of living that people want.

Indeed, nineteenth-century utilitarianism generally held that the government should not interfere in the bargaining between workers and the owners of capital, on the grounds that a free-market economy would actually yield the greatest good for the greatest number.

Hate supermarkets?

- Should there be free competition in the retail grocery sector?
- Is competition always to the benefit of the consumer?

In Britain, where there is a danger of unfairness in the way that a particular sector of the market is working, the Competition Commission can be requested to carry out an examination of the way things are working, and whether as a whole it operates in the interest of the consumer. In particular, it can assess whether one or more companies hold such a dominant position in the market that they distort the freedom of consumers to choose what to buy or of other companies to compete effectively.

If a company is successful, in capitalist terms, it will yield profits for its owners (or shareholders) and this will involve being competitive by controlling costs and so on. Smaller businesses are unlikely to be able to compete with those that are larger and therefore have more clout in the marketplace.

Those who enjoy the benefit of good local shops can opt to use them. Those who are only concerned with convenience or price will go wherever it suits them. Ultimately, the market determines who wins and who loses.

- That is the basis of the free market. Does that make it fair?
- Success is not a political feature, but an economic one. But whether economics should be the only consideration is a political question.

An additional feature of the economics of food is that the spending power of the major supermarket chains means that they can drive down the prices they pay their suppliers. Some of these are among the poorest in the world. A report in 2007 from Action Aid found that workers in Bangladeshi garment factories could be paid as little as 5p an hour, and Indian workers processing cashew nuts only 30p a day.

- The free-trade argument would be that trade is the best way out of poverty, and that low wages are better than none. Whilst acknowledging that the bulk of the profit on each item goes to the supermarket, free-traders would say that this system is still to everyone's benefit in the long run.
- The counter argument is that such trade arrangements effectively trap the poorest in their poverty, and that more responsibility needs to be taken on the part of supermarkets to ensure that their suppliers treat their workers fairly.
- Trade is seldom free, of course. Agricultural subsidies and the system of tariffs and quotas ensures that a certain measure of control and protection is given to producers in the developed world, at the expense of third-world producers. Free-traders would see this as unjust.
- Finally, however, there is the simple fact that people like to buy cheap clothes and food, and, if they continue to do so, aware of the source of such goods, then they implicitly approve of the trade done by the supermarket. The choice of goods marked 'Fairtrade' enables shoppers to register that they want to buy in a way that is fair to the original supplier. As with organic food, the economics of the retail market mean that if the public are willing to pay more, it will happen.

Socialists might argue that industries should be nationalized, so that everyone, rather than just the shareholders, profit. On the other side, a neo-liberal or conservative view of this would be that efficiency and profit is the incentive which drives business forward, and which ends up benefiting everyone involved. Both arguments are utilitarian.

Clearly, fair competition between companies is thought to be good from a utilitarian perspective, but where competition is deemed *unfair*, it would seem that, by regulating the degree of market dominance allowed, governments may ensure that utilitarianism trumps capitalism – since the benefit to the majority takes precedence over the right of a company to dominate the market.

Issues for utilitarianism

When we say that everyone should have the best possible health care or a reasonable standard of living in retirement, we are not making a utilitarian assessment about what would benefit society as a whole, we are making a case for what we consider to be the reasonable expectation of the individual, and what would be considered a just arrangement for society. In other words, the judgement is based on an assessment of what constitutes a civilized life for the individual. It would be right to promote such a civilized life, even if society *as a whole* did not benefit from it. *In other words, there are some basic rights that should take precedence over general benefit.* A fundamental question for utilitarianism is therefore: Do human rights trump utilitarian benefits?

Another question: How do you assess who is involved, and therefore whose interests should be taken into account? Should that be done on a local basis, or in terms of the workforce of a particular company? Should it be regional or national? Indeed, should it be global?

When it comes to global warming or restrictions on international trade, the interests of the citizens of one country may well conflict with the overall interests of the global community. Which utilitarian assessment do you take into account – the local or the global?

The other side of this coin is the complaint that, in any utilitarian assessment, minorities get trumped by majorities, and are therefore discriminated against when it comes to taking their preferences into account.

This, of course, applies to both utilitarianism and democracy.

Issues for capitalism

Capitalism is essentially a mechanism for generating wealth, and it requires that the profit motive is primary. But unrestrained capitalism may produce results (conditions of working people, effects on the environment, etc.) that people find unacceptable. In other words, the social or environmental price of generating wealth for those who own capital may be seen as unacceptably high.

In practice then, looked at theoretically, political direction and free-market capitalism look incompatible, since the economic principles that drive capitalism are not political. However, most states feel the need to impose politically motivated legislation upon industry in the name of fairness, by anti-monopoly legislation, for example, or by rules that apply to the environmental impact of products, or their marketing (for example, restrictions on the advertising of tobacco products).

Marx saw working people threatened by alienation – for rather than being able to take pride in what they produced, they were reduced to cogs in an impersonal wheel of production. That is still a relevant threat, but along with it goes 'commodification' as all aspects of the individual's life is given monetary rather than personal value – from the job to the notion of fame, everything has its price and place.

Minimum wage/workplace regulation

The imposition of a legal minimum wage and restrictions on the conditions under which people are to be allowed to work, represent a political restriction on capitalism. Small businesses often complain about such restrictions and the amount of 'red tape' associated with them

If people are prepared to work for less than the legal minimum wage, should they not be allowed to do so? How do you encourage firms to offer better conditions of work? Should you vary the levels of tax on profits according to the quality of the work experience that a company provides? Is that too much interference in the operation of capitalism? Might it stifle competition?

Capitalism depends on success within markets, based on the technology required to produce and sell, and the information needed in order to do so. Neo-liberalism tends to free capitalism from restrictive legislation, on the assumption that the generation of profit is, in itself, a valid aim of business.

But are capitalism and utilitarianism capable of achieving fairness in society, or is something more needed?

Distributive justice

It is often assumed that the key feature of good government is its management of the economy. In other words, that what people want is an ever-increasing standard of living, and a government is put in power in order to deliver the goods. There are, of course, other factors – people want schools, hospitals, roads, security – but even the provision of these takes on economic and political significance, since the most wealthy are more likely to use private medicine, education and so on, whereas the poorer have no choice but to accept what the state supplies.

A key question asked of government, therefore, is whether it has provided services that reflect good value for money (money that the people have provided in taxes), on the assumption that the more efficient a government is, the less tax it will have to raise and the more money people keep in their own pockets.

But there are problems with this:

- In a global market, the economy of any one country is going to be heavily dependent upon what is happening elsewhere in the world. An individual government is not able to determine or able to counter global trends.
- Whether the economy should deliver higher standards of living is a political question which is not often asked, since its answer is assumed.
- It tends to assume that economic indicators (the inflation rate, level of employment and so on) are 'neutral' with respect to political decisions – and thus able to be used to compare the performance of governments. In fact, the very things that are used as a measurement are part of the political decision-making process.

Conservatism and socialism have tended to divide on this, with conservatives expecting to pay less tax, and accepting – where possible and appropriate – a reduction in services, allowing individuals freedom to choose how to spend the additional money they have available after tax. The socialist tendency, representing the particular concern for the poorer sections of society, has generally favoured better public services (on which those they represent depend) with, if necessary, increases in tax, which fall proportionately more heavily on the wealthy.

But how do you decide how goods should be distributed? Do you do so on the basis of:

• what people need?
• what people deserve?
• equal shares for all?

In theory, Marx held that people should give according to their ability and receive according to their needs. Is that a realistic aspiration? In terms of distributive justice, one thinker has dominated discussion for the last 30 years: John Rawls.

Rawls and fairness

The revival of interest in political philosophy itself in recent times is often seen as initiated by John Rawls's book *A Theory of Justice* (1972), and his view of 'justice as fairness' has been influential, not just by being agreed with, but by provoking responses from those who see things differently and are quick to point out its shortcomings. Rawls wanted to show that a broadly liberal-democratic view of the distribution of resources could be given firm and logical foundations. He was also critical of the application of utilitarianism to the issue of justice and fairness.

Rawls (1921–2002) presented a 'thought experiment' in order to get to grips with the logic of any redistribution of resources. Imagine a group of people gather together to decide how resources are to be distributed (he calls this the 'original position'). Each is able to say what is in his or her own best interest, but none of them knows who they are or what their position is in society. In other words, they do not know if they themselves are rich or poor. Rawls argues that each of them, since they will not know if they are in fact the poorest in society, will not want to legislate in any way that would adversely affect themselves if that were the case. He therefore argues that such people, thinking through the logic of their position will opt for two things:

1 That each person should have equal rights to the most extensive system of liberty, provided that it does not prevent others from having similar liberties.
2 That, if there are to be any inequalities in the distribution of resources, such inequalities should always be such as to benefit the least advantaged in society, and also that all should have a fair and equal opportunity to secure offices and positions.

Now there are a number of significant points to make about Rawls's argument. The first is that he clearly comes from a liberal democratic position, seeking freedom for all, whilst maintaining social justice in the distribution of wealth. What he seeks to do in his thought experiment is to frame a logically coherent framework to implement that wish.

In other words, rather as Immanuel Kant had argued that ethics should be based on the pure practical reason, without any thought of personal rewards or results, so Rawls is arguing that redistributing in favour of the poorest is what everyone would see as the logical thing to want, if they were not influenced by their own social position.

But it is also important to appreciate that Rawls is concerned as much with the process by which fairness is established as about the final result. He wants to show that it is possible, through pure logic and people's natural self-interest, to establish rules for a fair distribution in society without reference to any external authority.

Rawls's criticism of utilitarianism

What Rawls offers is a form of 'ideal contractualism' – a modern version of the 'social contract' theory of the seventeenth and eighteenth centuries – which he hoped would provide an alternative to utilitarianism. He believed that a social contract approach takes the individual more seriously than does utilitarianism, since it does not require an individual to sacrifice any benefit in favour of society as a whole. This, of course, is a major problem with utilitarianism, for majorities always seem to trump minorities.

But Rawls also felt that utilitarianism was at odds with our usual moral judgements. In other words, we have an intuitive view of what is implied by fairness which does not necessarily comply with the conclusion of a utilitarian assessment of benefits. This is a widely-held criticism of act utilitarianism – that there are occasions when a weighing of the potential benefits of a course of action to all those involved, does not give a result that a morally sensitive person finds acceptable.

Rawls therefore wanted to establish a 'reflective equilibrium' between the principles of justice and people's 'considered moral judgements'. He wanted his proposal for fairness to be compatible with firm moral traditions that people already held, and he has an underlying moral assumption that individuals deserve the right to equal respect. In other words, the 'original position' is not autonomous as a way of establishing principles of justice – for it depends on prior moral positions or 'intuitions'.

R. M. Hare (1919–2002) is one of those who felt that this rigged Rawls's argument to give anti-utilitarian conclusions which Rawls himself held from the start. In other words, Rawls works on basic assumptions that are part of the modern liberal democratic tradition, and then devises an artificially contrived situation that attempts to establish them on the basis of pure logic.

Problems with Rawls's 'original position'

Here is a major problem: *Thought experiments are just that; they do not reflect what happens in real life.* There never was and never will be a situation in which people do not know their place in society, and of course Rawls never suggested that there could be. But does that attempt to construct an unreal situation in order to show the logic of self-interest give a result that can be translated into the real world? This question lies behind a criticism of Rawls from a **communitarian** standpoint.

Communitarians argue that people are always embedded in society; that we are who we are because of our place in our community, what we do, how we relate to others and so on. Hence you cannot meaningfully take from people the awareness of who they are, for that is essential for any form of political awareness and decision-taking. Hence the decisions taken by those in Rawls's 'original position' may sound logical, but they cannot reflect what actually happens when people get together.

That does not mean that people might not, for altruistic reasons, opt for a form of justice that does not benefit them personally – but if they do so, they do so with their eyes open. In actual fact, many people might want to take a risk – to opt for a situation where, if they are better off, they can benefit still further. They may reckon that the risk of losing out is worth taking. In some ways this is typical of the entrepreneur within a capitalist system, reckoning that it is better to take a risk in the hope of making a greater profit, rather than playing safe and making very little.

Hence, even if Rawls's logic is sound, it is not and can never be, the sort of logic that real people in real political situations can use.

Fair opportunities

A very different approach from that of Rawls was taken by Robert Nozick in *Anarchy, State and Utopia* (1974), another hugely influential book. Nozick's view is that priority should be given to the right of individuals to generate wealth and retain it for themselves. He thinks it is wrong for the state to impose equality by taxing those who have made money in order to contribute to services for those in need. Nozick argues that it is perfectly all right to give to someone if you so choose, but not to have society force you to contribute. This, of course, reflects a strong tradition of charity giving in the United States. Where state taxation and provision are less, the opportunity for individual moral responsibility to provide for people increases.

Whereas Rawls thought that you could abstract people from their background in order to get some ideal view about principles of justice, Nozick argued that it was important to include the historical acquisition of property in assessing justice. In other words, he recognized that a key feature of who someone is, is reflected in what they possess and in how they came to possess it. Also, the abilities that someone has are linked with their background, education, opportunities in society and so on. So it is difficult to see how any justice can be established unless the economic and social background of individuals is taken into account.

Fairness is a philosophical concept, based on the understanding of how the different parts of society work together, what they need, and how they can flourish. Sounds familiar? Of course – for here we are back with Plato and his threefold division of society. For all the limitations of Plato's *The Republic*, at least it recognized that different people have different needs.

And should those who have the natural ability to succeed beyond that of their fellows be prevented from flexing their economic and political muscles? Even if all were equally provided for, they would not remain economically equal for long. Here we are back with Nietzsche and his sense of humankind being in the forefront of evolution, moving forward and aspiring to overcome itself, working towards the arrival of the *übermensch* and the next stage of evolution.

Absolute equality may sound fine, but how would you give people the incentive to work and contribute as much as they can, if they receive the same in return, whatever the value of their contribution? Is it natural that people should expect to receive the benefits of their contribution and consider that to be only fair?

Equality of self-direction and moral regard

Equality is a foundational concept for much political debate and political philosophy. The American Declaration of Independence of 1776 claimed 'all men are born equal' as the starting point for setting up its political system. We have already considered distributive justice as a way of treating people equally, but what else is implied by it?

There are different forms of equality:

- Equality of opportunity – even if people end up in different positions in terms of wealth and achievement, because of their differences in abilities or intelligence, they should all have the same opportunities presented to them. Thus, for example, access to schooling or job opportunities should be open equally to everyone.
- Equality of goods – this has already been considered, and suggests that people should receive an equal share of resources. In practice, of course, except in the most restricted of communities, such equality cannot be maintained for long, because people make very different use of whatever resources they are given.
- Equality of rights – that there are basic rights offered to all alike, such as the right to life, liberty and the pursuit of

happiness, or freedom from persecution on grounds of colour, race, religion and so on.

- Equality of respect – however different people may be in their abilities, they may all receive the same degree of respect, simply by being a member of the human species.
- Equality of representation – the idea that everyone should have the same opportunity to vote, or in any other way take part in the process of government. Thus, for example, a Member of Parliament will claim that he or she is available to all his or her constituencies equally. Not all will avail themselves of that availability, but at least it is offered.

These various aspects of equality contribute to two very basic requirements for a fair and equal society – equality of *self-direction* and of *moral regard*. The first of these is the right of an individual to decide how he or she should live, and to take actions as far as possible, to put in place life-plans that aim at giving self-fulfilment.

Not all philosophers have argued for this. Aristotle claimed that women and slaves were not able to reason, or at least to reason effectively (in the case of women), and therefore they needed to be directed by men. Indeed, the thrust of his argument is that they will benefit from this, and lead happier lives, since they are supplied with an organized way of living that they would not be able to organize if left to their own devices. This view continues to be found wherever an authority claims to know what is in the interests of an individual, even if it is not what he or she wants.

Equality of moral regard is essential for establishing a fair way of dealing with those who are most vulnerable. In considering a person's rights, and the moral obligation of society towards them, it is crucial that who they happen to be is disregarded. Hence, it should make no difference morally, whether the person under consideration is young or old, male or female, a citizen or an illegal immigrant – all should have equal moral consideration.

For example

If an illegal immigrant is being exploited, the fact that the person is working illegally should not mean that they are not entitled to the protection offered by the law against that exploitation. The issue of their illegal status may need to be considered subsequently, but it should not prevent that equality of moral regard.

Another way of expressing the scope of equality within political discussion is simply to say that people should be treated with *equal consideration*.

Monochrome conformity

John Stuart Mill, surveying nineteenth-century England in his discussion of freedom, observed a rather sad fact about the majority of people:

> Comparatively speaking, they now read the same things, listen to the same things, see the same things, go to the same places, have their hopes and fears directed to the same objects, having the same rights and liberties and the same means of asserting them ... All the political changes of the age promote it, since all tend to raise the low and lower the high. Every extension of education promoted it, because education brought people under common influences. Improvement in the means of communication promotes it ... Increase of commerce and manufacture promotes it ... The ascendancy of public opinion ... forms so great a mass of influence hostile to individuality that in this age the mere example of non-conformity, the mere refusal to bend a knee to custom, is itself a service.
>
> *On Liberty* (p. 83)

The influence of the global media in the twenty-first century has increased this pressure to conform. This might seem a major problem with the quest for equality and fairness – where all receive the same treatment, the same opportunities and are bombarded with the same advertising, individuality and eccentricity are threatened.

Whether that is in fact the case is open to debate; some might claim that 'difference' is celebrated more than conformity in most liberal democracies. But it serves as a warning that, even if there is no attempt to impose absolute equality, there is a natural tendency for education and capitalism to promote it.

The most dangerous situation, of course, is one where equal consideration depends on political conformity, since any government operating on that basis offers benefits only to those who show unquestioning allegiance to its particular point of view.

Web 2

It is interesting to reflect on the equality offered by the social networking sites on the internet. Individuals can now publish and share information about themselves and interact with others wherever they are on the globe. While this reflects a newly created zone of equal opportunity, it also preserves – indeed celebrates – individuality. The internet, perhaps for the first time, provides a space in which huge numbers of people can interact with one another, while preserving their own identity and individuality.

Citizens or consumers?

Hannah Arendt (1906–75) was concerned to explore the modern equivalent of the Greek '*polis*', namely a society in which people could act together as equals and become engaged in the political process. She commented on the danger in modern society of allowing individuals to be treated as consumers rather than citizens. In other words, they are reduced to passive recipients of whatever the government considers to be in their best interest, rather than active participants in the political process itself.

If management of the economy is key to political success, economic well-being is the key to voter satisfaction, and voter satisfaction is the key to remaining in power. But is that an adequate basis for political decision-making in a democracy? The danger, where a 'consumer' approach is taken, is that people will be assumed to be controllable and conformist, provided that they are promised suitable material gains in return for their support in the polls.

Not for long!

In this chapter, we have so far been concerned with how goods should be distributed in order to establish a sense of fairness in society. But there are some philosophers – for example Ronald Dworkin (b.1931) – who point out that, however fairly the sharing out of goods in some original position might be, that fairness will not last for long, because some people will be more skilled than others in trading what they have. Those who are industrious might reasonably claim that they deserve the extra resources that they accumulate, and that it would be wrong to re-distribute them. But other factors come into play – one person may be struck down with illness, a freak storm may damage the home of another, a harvest may fail. These unpredictable factors will start to create inequalities. Of course, one person may choose to insure against such unpredictable happenings, while another may not. Is the uninsured person thereby contributing to his or her future plight? If so, it would be unreasonable to complain if some unpredictable but insurable event occurs.

This recognition of the way in which fortunes change strengthens the view that people cannot really be abstracted from the communities and world in which they live. In an uncertain world, a redistribution of resources cannot preserve equality for long.

Democracy

This term is derived from the Greek word *demos* (people) and *kratos* (power). It is 'people power' in the sense that people are able to choose and change a government by a process of election.

Democracy would seem to be the logical expression of equality. It asserts that every adult in a society, provided that he or she qualifies in some basic way, is able to express a view about the way society is governed. Just as Bentham's principle of utility argued that the right thing to do was what offered the maximum benefit to the greatest number, so a democracy is the right form of government, according to utilitarianism, since it conforms to the wishes of the majority.

Or is it? In Aristotle's day, democracy was only for a male minority; women and slaves had no say in government. And his justification for that was simply that participation should be limited to those capable of making informed judgements, and that required the ability to reason and a measure of financial security. Although Kant favoured democracy, he never considered that it should extend down to wage labourers, and thought that nobody should vote who did not earn his own living by business or profession. And Nietzsche felt that democracy would hold back the development of the strong. Looking at the effectiveness of holding power, as set out by Machiavelli in *The Prince*, one may wonder whether power is best exercised by those in the precarious situation of always being at the mercy of the people at the next election.

Plato disliked democracy because it appeared to him to be mob rule – now it has become the political option of choice. Indeed, it is often assumed that, once freed from the imposition of military or religious dictatorships, nations will automatically follow the wishes of the people and establish democracies. In practice, however, once established, democracy is carefully 'managed' by the government of the day. Voters are made promises, they are bombarded with advertisements from contending political parties, their choices are limited, and the outcome is statistically predictable, once a general tendency in voting has become apparent.

A crucial question for democracy: *How do you protect the welfare of minorities?* If a simply democratic vote decides what will happen, then a minority – almost by definition – is going to lose out. Perhaps the assumption is that people will be in a majority for some issues and a minority for others. But that still means that, generally, the majority will get its way.

One possibility is that you have a constitution that requires an overwhelming majority vote in order to deprive a minority of its rights, but although that may modify the perceived injustice, it does not remove it.

Regional assemblies may solve the problem where geographical differences between electors are seen as crucial – thus, it is important for those living in Northern Ireland, Wales or Scotland to have a measure of political independence, and an assembly for their own part of the nation, rather than having all issues decided in a parliament that will always, by virtue of the numbers involved, be dominated by England.

Aided by the popular press, majorities may dominate minorities, which is a clear issue for any democratic or utilitarian system. But informed agreement is equally confusing. In a modern democracy (where voting is done through the proxy of focus groups and opinion polls most of the time), the outcome of issues depends to a considerable extent on the way in which they are presented by the government, and whether there is an alternative view to be presented by opposition parties. In other words, public opinion is always open to 'spin'. Facts are more difficult to establish, and it is assumed that only a few people will know all the facts and issues on any one topic.

Citizens' juries

In both Britain and the USA (where they originated) citizens' juries gather groups of people to discuss policy ideas put forward by the government. Whether those ideas are developed further depends on the reactions to them on the part of the juries. Those who serve on the juries can call witnesses and hear evidence before giving their own verdict on the policy under discussion.

- Do they give people a genuine say in what is to happen?
- What is the difference between a jury and a focus group?
- Is this genuine democracy in action, and likely to engage more people in the political process?
- How else might individuals play a more direct role in the process of democratic decision-making?

Governments are there to *persuade* people. If they have a working majority, a political party supporting a government need not be unduly concerned about short-term adverse poll ratings – but when it becomes sustained, or an election is approaching, is there added pressure to present and sell issues in a way that will please the electorate?

Single issue voting

A referendum provides a check on the process of representative democracy. In a referendum, everyone is able to vote on a specific issue – thus getting around the problem of establishing whether representatives elected to parliament are able to reflect accurately the wishes of the electorate. It is the nearest a modern political system gets to the original form of simple democracy.

However, there is a fundamental difference between a modern referendum and original democracy – namely that the *framing of the question to be put to people can influence the way in which they vote*. There is no scope for the discussion of the issue across the whole electorate, with a view to providing a subtle answer to the matter in hand. It remains a rather crude yes/no decision, and hence is open to manipulation and media influence. Seldom are political options able to be resolved by a simple choice, and people may vote the same way for many different reasons.

Democracy can mean many things. To Plato it was rule by an unthinking majority. To the 'social contract' proponents in the eighteenth century, it was the new voice of the people in establishing their control over government. Today, representative democracies are, in general, carefully managed, manipulated and predictable systems of government – hovering between centralized government by a professional political elite, and government by the occasional whim of a minority of people in marginal constituencies.

06

freedom

In this chapter you will learn:
- about negative and positive freedom
- to consider whether free speech should be limited
- about Mill's view that you should be free to do what you like, provided you harm nobody else.

Freedom is probably the most fundamental and crucial concept in political philosophy. Everyone agrees that freedom is a good thing, but it raises many questions:

- What is the purpose of being free?
- Do I simply want society to impose no restraints on what I can do?
- Do I want to be free to plan out my life as I wish?
- How does my desire for freedom square with the very clear need for some sort of political and social order?
- If what I want to do conflicts with the interests of others, how is my freedom to do it going to be reconciled with their freedom to stop it?

If there were no problems with freedom, there would probably be no need for political philosophy or, indeed, politics. We have an issue because it is clear that, in a complex society, people cannot simply do their own thing without recognizing that what they do impacts on others, and that they are impacted upon in return. Hence, politics is a way of negotiating between ordered constraint and freedom of the individual.

- How is the idea of liberty related to the need for law and for political control?
- Where is the line to be drawn between things that should be left to the individual and things where conformity to the state is the best option?

Clearly, complete freedom for everyone would lead to chaos and anarchy (in the common meaning of that term), and it would be incompatible with the complex nature of society – you cannot organize education, health care, defence, and so on, if everyone is free to do whatever they like, because all those things depend on people being predictable and conforming to basic rules to enable society to work. On the other hand, nobody would consider it right for people to behave like ants, obeying fixed rules and dedicating all their energy unthinkingly to the benefit of the colony as a whole. The severest criticism of some socialist and communist states is that they have attempted, for the general good, to deny people freedom to live as they choose. Clearly, there has to be a balance.

Forget determinism ...

The freedom debate within political philosophy is not the same as the more general argument about determinism. Is a virus 'free'? Is a tree 'free' to grow? From a scientific perspective, every event is conditioned by antecedent causes. There is a good argument for the idea that everything we ever do is determined by the past. In that sense we are never free, and never can be.

But that is not the sense in which we are to consider freedom here. For our purposes we are concerned with people's experience of being free to choose what to do. We need to assume that, without externally imposed rules, they will be free.

Except (and this is a very big 'except'), there have been those (notably Hegel and, following him, Marx) who have argued that the process of change within society has an historical inevitability, and that what might be experienced as free choice is simply our own working out of a process of change that can be measured and predicted. Individual freedom can then be restricted on the basis that, if people were aware of the tides of historical change, they would understand that what feels like an imposed restriction is in fact inevitable.

For now, however, we will set this particular option aside, and concentrate on the experienced freedom of an individual within the political system.

The basic question is simply: *Why should I accept anyone else telling me what to do? Why should I not simply do what I like?*

This leads towards a *negative* definition of freedom – in other words, freedom is what is left to you once other people's interference in your life is taken into account. In its *positive* sense, however, freedom is about choosing how to live, what to do, and the ability to set our own agenda and goals.

These two senses of freedom – negative freedom and positive freedom – were famously set out by Isaiah Berlin in a lecture entitled 'Two Concepts of Liberty', delivered at the University of Oxford in 1958, and itself a very good starting point for anyone interested in political philosophy.

Negative freedom

This is freedom from those things that limit what we can do. Philosophers who concentrate on this form of freedom attempt to define the minimum freedom that should be allowed to individuals in order for them to maintain their dignity as human beings. It is freedom 'from' rather than freedom 'to'.

John Stuart Mill (1806–73), whose work *On Liberty* is a key text for considering this approach to freedom, suggested that human creativity would be crushed without a suitable level of freedom. Isaiah Berlin disagreed with this, arguing that creativity can flourish even within the most repressive of regimes. This is a crucial point, because if Mill is right, then freedom 'from' restraints is absolutely essential if you are to have the freedom 'to' express and develop yourself as a creative individual. On the other hand, if Berlin is right, then an awareness of the 'freedom to' can enable positive and creative living, even in those situations where external conditions are harsh and restrictive.

Mill's 'harm' principle

Mill recognized that not every society was ready for its individual members to take responsibility for freedom in the way he was about to propose. In the case of what he calls 'backward' states:

> Despotism is a legitimate mode of government in dealing with barbarians, provided the end be their improvement, and the means justified by actually effecting that end.

> Liberty, as a principle, has no application to any state of things anterior to the time when mankind have become capable of being improved by free and equal discussion.

> from *On Liberty*

In other words, up to the point at which they can act as autonomous, thinking individuals, all that people need is a benign ruler who will tell them what to do.

For reflection

- How do you judge when a society or individuals within it are sufficiently mature and autonomous to accept the freedoms that Mill is about to recommend for them?
- Are most people really ready to exercise their freedom responsibly? What about children, or the senile, or those with major emotional or psychological problems, or those with a very low IQ?
- Mill pointed out that in Ancient Greece the rulers thought it appropriate to issue guidelines for how people should behave and what they should think. Mill was against that – in a civilized society, people should be free to make up their own minds. To impose an idea on others is to assume that you are infallible, and that is simply not the case.
- Contrast this with Plato – who thought that the philosophers should be able to control and tell people what to do. Plato felt that it was the responsibility of rulers to guide people in a way that was to their own good.

Mill wanted to maximize freedom. He argued that:

> ... the only purpose for which power can be rightfully exercised over any member of a civilized community, against his will, is to prevent harm to others. His own good, either physical or moral, is not a sufficient warrant.

Because:

> Over himself, over his own body and mind, the individual is sovereign.

In other words, even if you think that it would be to someone's benefit, or long-term happiness, that they should be compelled to do something, or refrain from doing something, that is insufficient reason for interfering. Even if one can see that someone is going to harm themselves, they must not be stopped from exercising their freedom from doing so. The only limitation is that they should not be permitted to *harm* anyone else. A person should be free to plan their life to suit their own character, and have complete liberty of 'tastes and pursuits', even if others think them 'foolish, perverse, or wrong.'

Smoking on trains

Following the UK ban on smoking on trains in 2007, Charles Kennedy, former leader of the Liberal Democrats, was caught having a smoke on a journey from Paddington to Plymouth. He wrongly argued that he was allowed to light up, provided that he leant out of the window to do so.

- Mill would probably have been on Kennedy's side – since he was directing the smoke outside the train, and therefore only harming himself.
- On the other hand, the legislation equally took Mill's line in that, overall, the freedom to smoke detracts from the freedom of other passengers to breathe smoke-free air.

On this basis, Mill argues for liberty of conscience, thought and feeling, and of expression, and also the freedom to unite together. In other words, you should be freely allowed to think, speak and act as an individual – and gather other people together to do, think or act – provided that no harm is done to others in the process …

> The only freedom which deserves the name, is that of pursuing our own good in our own way, so long as we do not attempt to deprive others of theirs, or impede their efforts to obtain it.

Free speech …

> If all mankind minus one were of one opinion, and only one person were of the contrary opinion, mankind would be no more justified in silencing that one person than he, if he had the power, would be justified in silencing mankind.

On Liberty

A key feature of Mill's view of liberty is freedom of speech, of which the quotation above is the clearest and most extreme expression. However, there are certain restrains that might be placed upon it, in the light of his 'harm' principle – since the expression of a point of view can be taken as incitement to hatred or to revolution. Hence there are restrictions on the freedom of expression, devised to prevent offence being given on grounds of religion, race, gender, sexual proclivity or age.

The problem with this is to know exactly what might be deemed to cause offence or harm. What about humour or irony? Can a comedian not make reference to religion, gender, sex, race or age in a joke? Is the intention as important as the words used?

Ahmadinejad at Columbia University

In September 2007, the President of Iran, who had come to New York to speak at the United Nations, was invited to take part in a political debate at Columbia University. In the course of the debate he was attacked as a 'petty dictator'. But should he have been invited to the debate at all?

Comments reported in *The Independent* on 25 September, ranged from:

> I feel that he should have the right to speak. Demonizing him is not going to change anything in the world.

> (An Iranian-born student)

to:

> It is hard to say who is the greater moral monster, the President of Iran or the Dean of the University who has said he would have invited Hitler before the Second World War.

> (A professor of medicine)

Whatever the political differences between the USA and Iran, there is a fundamental issue of free speech and a willingness to debate. Is allowing debate to take place – even with 'enemies' – more or less harmful than refusing them a platform?

In November 2007, the Nobel Prize winning scientist, James Watson, whose pioneering work on DNA is universally acknowledged and admired, made some remarks suggesting that some racial groups had intelligence that was different from others. His speaking engagements in Britain were cancelled, and Ken Livingston, Mayor of London, said 'Such views are not welcome in a city like London' and Watson returned to the United States, saying that he wanted to try to save his job, having been suspended from his post in Spring Harbor Laboratory, Long Island (from which he subsequently resigned).

He had explained that he had not meant to imply that black people were less intelligent than white, and apologized unreservedly for any offence caused, but that was not enough to prevent the retribution. In an article in the *Observer* (21 October 2007) by Henry Porter, entitled 'His views are hateful. But so is the attempt to deny him a voice' Colin Blakemore, Professor of Neuroscience at Oxford, is quoted as saying 'Jim Watson is well-known for being provocative and politically incorrect. But it would be a sad world if such a distinguished scientist was silenced because of his more unpalatable views.'

So, in considering this situation, we need to balance Mill's 'harm' principle, with his insistence on freedom of speech – even for someone who is in a minority of one. However, Mill would restrict the freedom to express views in a situation where they are likely to stir up trouble. Hence he would have no problem with the idea of restricting free speech in a situation which was liable to 'incite to hatred' – indeed, he would see that as exactly the kind of situation which the law should intervene to prevent.

Objections to Mill

There are at least two fundamental objections to Mill's view of the freedoms that should be permitted to individuals. The first is:

• That every action may have an effect on others, even if we are quite unaware of what that effect might be. In other words, it is naïve of him to assume that what I do in the privacy of my own home is not of immediate concern to other people.

To take an extreme example, downloading child pornography is done privately, and it can be argued that the material is already available on the web, waiting to be purchased, and therefore the act of making this particular download does not materially harm anyone. Now the act of downloading might not affect anybody else, but it is regarded as a serious criminal offence, because the trade in child pornography is based on the sexual exploitation of children. The person who downloads the result is therefore implicated in its production, and therefore in the prior harm done to those children. In the same way, the private act of taking illegal drugs cannot be separated from the harm that may be caused to others through the exploitative nature of the drugs trade.

Hence, although those acts appear to be done in private, Mill's argument would still condemn them on the basis of the prior harms done. This does not deny that there may be situations where private activity should be permitted because it genuinely does not harm anyone else – it simply suggests that we need to be extremely careful when we try to draw the boundary between private acts and their public implications.

Recreational drugs

If you can smoke and drink excessively in the privacy of your own home, why should you not be free to use other drugs, too? After all, you would be potentially harming no one but yourself. The counter argument is that harm is done through the illegal trade that makes those drugs available.

But those who argue for the legalisation of all recreational drugs can then make the point that it is their *illegal* status that encourages the crime and exploitation involved in a black market. Hence the harm is done by the illegality, not by the drugs themselves.

But even if there were no illegal trade, should you be allowed to harm yourself? Should medical care be provided for those who deliberately contributed to their illness? Accounts of drug abuse frequently speak of the impact on friends and family, so should the 'harm' principle extend to them?

The second objection is even more fundamental, from the perspective of political philosophy:

- That the state *ought* to be concerned with the moral welfare of citizens; they should not be left to decide what they will do to themselves.

We have already noted that Plato and Aristotle thought that the state had a responsibility to provide the conditions under which people could lead the 'good life' – and therefore that questions determining the nature of such a 'good' life were rightly part of political philosophy.

For Mill, however, the responsibility that the Ancient Greeks gave to the state is now given to individuals. People are to determine *for themselves* what their 'good life' will be, and the task of the state is to allow them to pursue that good life by all means possible, provided that it does not restrict the ability of all others to do the same.

But was he right to place so much emphasis on the individual? Today we recognize that people's views are coloured by the media and by the general attitudes of society, and these may both be influenced by governments. Governments are expected to take views on health, the environment, education, civil disobedience, respect for authority and so on. But by doing so they are influencing the sphere of life that Mill might have regarded as the responsibility of the individual alone. Therefore, given the nature of the media and society, is it fair to ask if Mill's individualistic approach is still a realistic one?

Basic freedoms

Of course, the degree of freedom to be allowed to the individual depends on whether you think that people, left to their own devices, will work together harmoniously, in which case you can allow them maximum freedom. If, like the philosopher Hobbes, you sense that, in their natural state, it is every man for him/herself with resulting chaos, then you will probably want to constrain freedom rather more.

Benjamin Constant (1768–1830), writing in France following the Revolution and the rule of Napoleon, contrasted the 'Liberty of the Ancients' which were in effect the freedom to take part in republican political life, as exemplified in Ancient Greece and Rome, with the 'Liberty of the Moderns' which he set out in terms of those things which individuals could do without fear of government control or restraint.

In other words, he made the distinction between positive and negative freedom. For him, it was also a contrast between the attempt of the French Revolution to return to a republican tradition of civil life, which had not really achieved the freedom it had intended, and the 'Glorious Revolution' in Britain in 1688, which established the rule of law under a constitutional monarchy, guaranteeing basic freedoms to individual citizens. It is clear that, despairing of the former, Constant opted for the latter form of freedom. He sets out some basic freedoms, which are widely adopted as the minimum, namely, liberty of:

- religion
- opinion
- expression
- property.

He believed that society should protect each individual against punishment or constraint in those four things. Defining freedom in this way, of course, tends to promote an individualistic view of humankind – in other words, that we define ourselves mainly by what we as individuals choose to do, rather than seeing ourselves as small parts of a larger social whole.

As Constant was well aware, this is a tradition that developed in 'modern' times. If you go back to Ancient Greece, there was far more of a sense that the individual could only function and fulfil his or her purpose through participation in the whole social and political context. For Aristotle, man was a political animal, not an individual animal that just happened, for his own personal benefit, to agree with others about how to live together. But that, of course, is a matter of 'positive freedom' ...

Positive freedom

Positive freedom is the freedom to choose what we will do with our lives, to set goals and to work to achieve them. Should or can governments promote such freedom?

The danger with this approach, as presented by Berlin, is that there is a temptation to suggest that people should have a 'higher' freedom than that which they actually choose for themselves. In other words, it is tempting for those in power to suggest that people are ignorant of their own potential and best interests.

There is a danger of telling people that they are truly free, when what you have actually done is imposed upon them a notion of what they should be 'free' to do. And it is a short step from that to restraining people who have a lesser or more selfish notion of what they should be free to seek in life.

Berlin, in his lecture 'Two Concepts of Liberty', quotes Kant as saying 'Paternalism is the greatest despotism imaginable.' There is always the danger that a well-meaning reformer will come to treat people as material to be shaped by his chosen reforms, whether they choose to be so helped or not. And those imposed goals, and the imposed freedom to achieve them, is really just another form of control.

A clear example of the imposition of positive freedom is seen in the work of Rousseau. As we saw above (page 51), Rousseau argued that people's true happiness and freedom lay in setting aside their own particular wills and finding their true freedom by aligning themselves with the 'General Will' of the people. Rather than remaining slaves to their own passions and inclinations, they would then experience the freedom of giving themselves to the greater political enterprise. And, of course, if people did not recognize that their own best interest and freedom lay in that direction, they would have to be – in Rousseau's own chilling phrase – 'forced to be free'.

Mill opposed this approach

Mankind are greater gainers by suffering each other to live as seems good to themselves, than by compelling each to live as seems good to the rest.

(*On Liberty*, p. 18)

Berlin argues that, for a society to be free, it is essential that no rules are regarded as absolute. In other words, it is always the right of the individual to interpret and understand the rule as it applies to him or her, and nobody should be forced to act in an inhumane way. It is also important for such freedom to be based on a definition of what it is to be a human being. People need to be able to develop an idea of the end or purpose of human life; they should be free to consider and discuss this, and to modify it as seems appropriate. In the end, that is not something that can be imposed on people, it is something that they have to embrace for themselves.

What this amounts to …

I complain that I cannot do what I want, therefore I am not free. You tell me that I want the wrong things, and that if I managed to align my wants and goals with something else (namely what you think I should want) then I will be free to achieve them. *But is it freedom if I am only free to conform?*

Another more recent aspect of positive freedom (as proposed by the French socialist philosopher Gorz, see page 73) concerns the encouragement of participation in the political order (rather along the republican lines, as found in the Ancient Greek *polis*) by offering every citizen a payment, so that they would not need to be employed in order to enjoy and contribute to society. This suggests that we may not be free to do what we like because we are too busy earning money – freed from that need, we would be free to use our time more creatively.

On the other hand, the offering of such a freedom would cut across so many of the assumptions about work and the economic order, that it is difficult to see how it could be implemented without some wholesale change in society and its values.

School uniform

Where a uniform is required, freedom is …

- tying your tie very short
- hitching your skirt higher than generally permitted
- wearing odd socks
- wearing a shirt but no jacket on a freezing morning

(examples of pushing the boundaries of negative freedom).

Where no uniform is required, freedom is …

- coming to school dressed identically in jeans and tee shirts
- freely accepting the slavery of fashion

(examples of a limited attempt at positive freedom).

Effective freedom

It is important to distinguish between being legally allowed to do something, and actually being able to go and do it. A law could be passed allowing everyone, if they so wish, to run a mile in two minutes. That would not, however, increase their *effective* freedom, because, although allowed to do so, they are physically incapable of it. Having a minimum of restrictions and a maximum of possibilities is fine, but in the real world most people will never have the opportunity either to become all that they are allowed to become, or to need to be restrained from doing everything that is possible for them to do. Their effective freedom depends on actually having the means and ability to choose what to do.

This idea of effective freedom relates back to the consideration of fairness in Chapter 05. The quest for a fair society – whether through the sort of agreements suggested by Rawls, or through a utilitarian assessment of benefits – is at the same time a quest for a society in which *effective* freedom is maximized. To be treated unfairly is to have one's potential limited, and therefore to be denied things that would be possible if one had a fairer share of resources. Poverty is not just a matter of having insufficient money or resources, it is also about not being free to do the things that people with more money are freely able to choose to do.

Effective freedom is also improved if society is stable and well organized. In his essay 'On Civil Liberty', David Hume, concerned with the balance of freedom and authority, and surveying the benefits of different political forms, commented on how improved life had become under monarchies:

> It may now be affirmed of civilized monarchies, what was formerly said in praise of republics alone, *that they are a government of Laws, not of Men.* They are found susceptible of order, method, and constancy, to a surprising degree. Property is there secure, industry encouraged, the arts flourish, and the prince lives secure among his subjects, like a father among his children.

Although he does not believe that monarchy is an ideal form of government, here he is taking a pragmatic line. If laws are drawn up and applied fairly, and property is made secure, people are less likely to live in fear and thus their effective freedom is increased.

In other words ...

In order to be free, I need to feel secure. If I am constantly trying to guard and protect myself, I won't be able to plan and live life as I would wish.

Fear of freedom

The French existentialist philosopher Jean-Paul Sartre, argued that existence precedes essence – in other words, we do not have a fixed self to which we need to conform, but we construct who we are as we go through life.

But this brings with it a terrible responsibility, namely that we are free to choose not just what we shall do, but also who we shall become. For Sartre and other existential philosophers,

such as Martin Heidegger, this kind of freedom is something
from which many people will be tempted to run. It is a threat as
well as a challenge. It is far easier to adopt some fixed role or
mask than to be faced with the freedom to shape our own lives.

> **Grown up?**
>
> Negative freedom is that carved out by adolescents, pushing the
> boundaries of what parents will allow.
>
> Positive freedom is the scary prospect of being an adult, alone in
> the world and fully responsible for success or failure.

The 'triadic' alternative

Berlin's distinction between negative and positive freedom was
challenged in 1967 by an American legal philosopher, Gerald
MacCallum. He argued that these were two aspects of a single
concept. Freedom occurs when an agent is free from external
constraints so that he or she can do or become certain things.
This suggests that freedom is a 'triadic' concept, i.e. it is based
on *three* things: the agent, the thing or things that limit what the
agent can do, and what it is the agent *wants* to do.

In other words, we only seek the *freedom from constraints*
because we want to be *free to do something*. The experience of
freedom only makes sense if we are both 'free to' and 'free
from'. Perhaps that is why negative freedom (removing all
restraints) is so scary and confusing unless one has a definite
goal, and thus a reason to use such freedom creatively.

Freedom and the law

Both Rousseau and Kant argued that if laws were devised that
were entirely rational, they would give freedom, because they
would require people to do exactly what a rational person
would want to do for him/herself anyway. This assumes that
society is comprised of free individuals, each of whom is
autonomous and acts in a rational way, both for his or her own
benefit and in order to allow all others to do the same.

This is the ideal that lies behind Kant's ethics. The three forms
of his 'Categorical Imperative' are the criteria which, according

to pure practical reason, determine if something is morally right. They may be summarized as:

1 Something is right if, and only if, you can will that the principle (or maxim) upon which you act should be made a universal law – in other words, that everyone else should also be allowed to act on the same principles as yourself.

2 Act in such a way as to treat all others as ends in themselves, rather than as mere means to your own ends.

3 Act as though you were legislating for a kingdom of 'ends', in other words, a society where everyone is a free and autonomous individual.

Notice how this overall view of morality fits with ideas of freedom and the law. They form the rational principles that should guide the actions of a free and autonomous person, living in a society where everyone else is free and autonomous also. The law is compatible with freedom, because the law expresses fundamental rational principles which allow the same measure of freedom and respect for others that you would wish shown to yourself. If that is the case, then why do you need rules at all? Why not allow everyone to be free and allow their rationality to prevail?

This may be well argued as an *ideal* against which to measure the freedom allowed in actual societies, but is it ever going to be a realistic option?

The problem – and it is a problem that we shall see repeated many times in the study of political philosophy – is that people do not live up to the standards set for them by some philosophers. If everyone were fully rational and not motivated by irrational impulses or their physical or emotional needs, then society would work perfectly on rational lines, and nobody would sense that their freedom was being constrained. However, life is not like that; we have a problem simply because people act from irrational motives, whether internal to themselves or externally imposed.

Hence, in practice, the law generally acts in line with the 'negative' rather than the 'positive' approach to freedom – in other words, it sets boundaries to the scope of freedom given to an individual. Law becomes a necessary protection to guard against the failure of reason and morality.

Mill saw law as a restriction of liberty. In all situations where you can get along without the law, fine. If you cannot do so, then the law needs to be imposed sufficiently to prevent one person's liberty from causing harm to others. Hence, a liberal society is likely to want a minimum of law, and thus a minimal government.

In whose interest?

Legislation would seem to be necessary when reason fails to deliver an acceptable result. But in whose interest should law be framed? If there is a dispute, each side may appeal to a legislator to offer a settlement or compromise. But is it ever possible to be sufficiently detached to be able to frame laws that are – and are seen to be – absolutely fair?

So how do you decide between conflicting interests, where the freedom of one appears to preclude the freedom of the other?

Freedom for geese or humans?

In April 2006, Chicago City Council voted to make it illegal to prepare and sell foie gras in any of the city's restaurants, on the grounds that the geese were tortured by being force-fed through tubes to make their livers expand to 20 times their natural size. Chefs launched a campaign against this, arguing that such legislation would violate a fundamental human right of their customers to choose what to eat. At a special fundraising dinner, to defy the wishes of the local politicians, every dish contained some form of the unfortunate geese.

- Is it right to legislate on what would normally be considered matters of personal morality? Is that what local politics should be about?
- Do individuals have any absolute right to satisfy their personal preferences, if what they do (or in this case, eat) offends others?
- If foie gras eaters have that right, what about paedophiles, voyeurs or cannibals?
- If, in a democracy, a majority want foie gras banned, should that view prevail over the minority who want to eat it?
- To what extent should individuals be forced to do what is in the general interest of, in this case, geese?

Two years later, in April 2008, the ban was repealed in the interest of *consumer* choice!

And this dilemma applies equally to *smoking in public places*, or the *right to walk naked in public*, or *the recreational use of certain drugs*. Every act of legislation curtails freedom, but protects others from those who would want to exercise it. A parallel argument can be made about *whether it is right for a government to take a country to war if a majority of its citizens are against it*. All of these issues show the limits of a utilitarian or democratic process of decision-making.

Whether it is ever realistic to think that the law, or the government, can determine what I would freely want for myself if I were thinking rationally and objectively, may depend on a fundamental problem for philosophy. *Is society basically just a collection of individuals, or are individuals created by the society within which they live?*

- The first may seem obvious, and can lead to arguments about whether there is any such thing as society, over and above people and their families.
- The second possibility becomes reasonable once we recognize that almost everything we do, or think, or desire, comes as a result of communication or sharing in society. I could never aspire to be a doctor if I lived in a social vacuum – for being a doctor is about dealing with other people who are sick, the whole social notion of medicine, the way that it is funded and so on. So what appears to be an individual choice is in fact a socially conditioned option.

Freedom is always freedom *within* a society, it is a freedom to develop in ways that society may have suggested to me (positive freedom) and in ways that it allows (negative freedom) – but either way, it is a social phenomenon. *Solitary freedom is like the Zen notion of one hand clapping!*

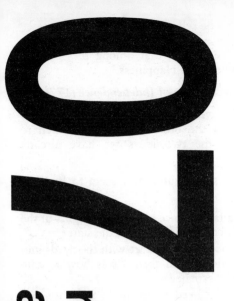

07
rights, justice and the law

In this chapter you will learn:
- about the balance between the individual and the state
- to consider what rights an individual should have
- about the limits of the law and of political authority.

'We hold these truths to be self-evident, that all men are created equal, that they are endowed by their Creator with certain unalienable Rights, that among these are Life, Liberty and the pursuit of Happiness.'

The American Declaration of Independence (1776)

The view that individuals have rights that should be upheld by law is a central feature of the broadly liberal approach to politics and is based on the two ideas we have already considered: equality and fairness.

But however 'self-evident' some truths may seem to be, they raise questions:

- How do you establish a fair balance between the rights of the individual and the political requirements of the state?
- How do you define justice? Do you start with the needs and aspirations of the individual and then assess how a state should enable them to be satisfied?
- Or do you start with the need to maintain a secure and prosperous state, and then assess what part individuals should be allowed or encouraged to play within it?
- And since control is exercised by law (or by brute force, if law breaks down) how do you ensure the independence of the judiciary, so that the law is not simply a tool of control in the hands of political leaders?

There are a whole range of issues here, but in this chapter we can touch on only some of them.

Justice handed down?

In *The Republic*, Plato argued that justice would benefit everyone in society; it was not simply a way of protecting the weak from the strong by offering them rights. Promoting justice was the result of seeing 'the Good' itself, rather than being swayed by the passing interplay of events – the shadows on the back wall of the prisoners' cave.

But Plato thought that justice could not be understood by everyone, but only by those who were suitably educated. The responsibility of the Guardians was therefore to grasp and hand down justice to the unenlightened. Individuals could flourish only if the state were well ordered, and if a 'noble lie' about the status of the lower orders was needed in order to keep them in their place, such bending of the truth was a price worth paying.

In other words, for Plato, justice and law were handed down to people from the Guardians, who alone knew what was in the people's own best interest and that of the *polis*.

Aristotle, equally, saw justice as the result of education in the virtues of tolerance and respect, but he also considered that the truest form of justice was a kind of friendship – in other words, a mutual exchange that could promote human flourishing. But he was realistic about who, in the *polis*, could establish such justice. In *Politics*, Book IV, he suggests that the state should be ruled by the middle classes, since the well-born tended to be arrogant and the poor to commit petty crimes, while the middle classes were more susceptible to rational argument!

So when it came to rights, justice and the law, the Greeks were concerned primarily with the state rather than with the individual. You simply could not trust the majority of people to set their own laws. Citizens could take part in debates and vote, of course, but that process was not open to everyone, and although both would have accepted that a bad ruler might need to be overthrown, neither Plato nor Aristotle would have sanctioned lightly any form of public revolt.

Natural subordination?

The clear implication of this argument is that some are more naturally suited to rule than others, and that people should know their place and keep to it. It is claimed that, by each taking an appropriate role in society, based on inequality and natural subordination, all will benefit.

This is very different from the democratic approach but, since in modern democracies a majority does not take an active part in politics, is it not in fact what happens? A minority of professional politicians and civil servants take decisions and then (with whatever spin is necessary) explain them to the people. Although preserving an appearance of democratic equality, one might argue that such a situation is not so different from that of Ancient Greece.

So who determines justice? What happens when a military dictatorship imposes rule, claiming that it does so in order to prevent civil unrest and chaos? Who can decide between rulers and people? And where there is long-term confrontation between rulers and people, can the state really be secure?

And who controls truth in such a situation? Plato sanctioned the 'noble lie' about the invariable nature of the three classes of society. But what about a 'noble lie' about all civil unrest being the result of criminal elements or foreign trouble makers?

Military crackdown

Following the pro-democracy demonstrations in Burma during the last week of September 2007, the military junta clamped down on the protests. Monasteries were surrounded by troops, preventing the monks from continuing to take part in the demonstrations, parks were closed, the internet was disrupted, as were mobile phone connections. Troops fired on crowds using rubber bullets and tear gas. Live rounds were also used, and people were killed.

Other freedoms that were curtailed included the freedom of speech and the freedom of association – any groups gathering together in a public place were swiftly disbanded by the military.

The last time there were demonstrations on this scale was in 1988 when 3000 people were killed. Burma has been under military rule for 45 years. A military regime can control the country by using fear and the naked use of force where necessary. It seems impervious to the international condemnation of its actions, and a UN call for additional sanctions against the regime was vetoed by China, a key trading partner with Burma.

- How stable is such a regime? Eventually, where a people are kept in check through the threat of violence, a smaller and smaller number of people at the heart of the military tend to receive a disproportionate benefit to the disadvantage of almost everyone else. There can sometimes be a very rapid break up of the power base in such situations, with the potential for a return to democracy.

It is interesting to observe that the military used old-style physical force to put down the demonstrations, whereas the demonstrators and others used modern technology – determined to smuggle out information about what was happening through mobile phones and the internet. Technology facilitates the spread of information beyond national boundaries.

Justice from the people

Article 21 of the United Nations Declaration on Human Rights states that: 'The will of the people shall be the basis of the authority of government.' In other words, it endorses democracy as the system of government best able to deliver human rights. And this follows from the whole 'Social Contract' approach, which we examined in Chapter 03. Governments are set up through the agreement of the people, and part of that agreement is that individuals accept that they will be bound by the law that the government makes.

Governments establish political authority and impose that authority through law – that is a key feature of the internal stability and security of a state. The fundamental question to ask of a democratic system therefore is this: *To what extent is the law therefore produced by the people, as opposed to being imposed upon them?*

We shall return to this question later, in considering the place of legislation. For now, we need to keep in mind the fundamental issue of principle here – that within a democracy, it is the people who, through their elected representatives, shape what laws are passed. In addition, of course, we have the principle that the application of justice through the courts is separate from the executive power of government. This is designed to give added protection from the arbitrary use of government power.

Notice that, from a liberal democratic point of view, justice is agreed between people, and may be applied on a utilitarian basis – laws are aimed at expressing the wishes of the majority of the people. This leaves out of account any question of what constitutes the good life, or human flourishing, and whether law can contribute to this. In a democracy, the government is not expected to improve the people, but to do what they want.

Rights

- What are the basic rights that every individual should be entitled to?
- How can those rights best be protected?
- Under what circumstances, and for what reason, should a state remove the rights of individuals? (For example, someone who has committed a crime, or is a danger to the public, might have the right of personal liberty removed, by being put in prison.)

In August 1789, the National Assembly of France, 'believing that the ignorance, neglect, or contempt of the rights of man are the sole cause of public calamities and of the corruption of governments', set out its *Declaration of the Rights of Man*, the first article of which declared that 'Men are born and remain free and equal in rights' and those 'natural' rights were said to be: freedom, property, security, and the right to resist oppression.

The rights that are set out in that declaration remain familiar: people are to be considered innocent until proven guilty; authority resides with the whole state, and not with factions; people have the right to security, property and freedom of speech. The general sense of the declaration is that the individual is to be protected and given freedom and autonomy, free from the arbitrary exercise of power and protected by the law.

A few years earlier, as the American colonies were on the verge of declaring their independence from Britain, an American political campaigner, Thomas Paine (1737–1809), shot to fame through the publication of a pamphlet entitled *Common Sense*. He called for independence for the colonies, throwing off the monarchy and establishing a new republican government which would provide a more equal distribution of wealth, getting rid of the privileges of the gentry. A political system, he argued, should be based on reason and democracy. His pamphlet sold 150,000 copies!

But Paine is best known for his book *The Rights of Man*, published in two parts in 1791 and 1792 – a radical attack on *Reflections on the Revolution in France*, which had been published the previous year by the British conservative political thinker, Edmund Burke (1729–97). Although Burke had supported the independence of the American colonies, he was critical of the revolution in France, and argued for gradual change in society and the preservation of established tradition, rather than revolution. He also accepted a system of natural subordination. This, Paine could not tolerate.

Opposed to all rule by power or religious authority, Paine argues that the basis for political life should be a social compact – an agreement *between people* to work for the common good (rather than between the people and their government), since people exist before governments:

The fact therefore must be, that the individuals themselves, each in his own personal and sovereign right, entered into a compact with each other to produce a government: and this is the only mode in which governments have a right to arise, and the only principle on which they have a right to exist.

From *The Rights of Man* (second part)

He supported the claims of the French Declaration of the Rights of Man, particularly in the exercise of the 'natural rights of every man' – the only limits to freedom being that one should not thereby impede others from exercising a similar freedom (exactly the argument that Locke had made). It had also made the point that the law should only prohibit those things that are hurtful to society, and therefore nobody should be prevented from doing anything that is not specifically prohibited by the law, nor should they be required to do anything that is not set down in law.

Paine made an important distinction between 'natural rights' (as they had been proclaimed by the French) and 'civil rights':

• Natural rights – 'are those which appertain to a man in right of his existence. Of this kind are all the intellectual rights, or rights of the mind, and also all those rights of acting as an individual for his own comfort and happiness.'
• Civil rights – 'are those which appertain to man in right of his being a member of society. Every civil right has for its foundation, some natural right pre-existing in the individual. But to the enjoyment of which his individual power is not, in all cases, sufficiently competent. Of this kind are all those which relate to security and protection.'

From *The Rights of Man* (second part)

Natural rights?

We need to pause to consider what is meant by a 'natural' right. There are no rights in nature. The wildebeest, chased by lions, escapes into the river only to be devoured by crocodiles. There is no court to which the poor creature can appeal against being eaten. Life and death are determined by physical nature, strength and cunning. The strongest survive and breed, and thus each species develops.

The whole idea that people have rights which they can use to argue against some injustice done to them is the product of the system of agreements and laws that are established within the state. Rights and the law, and indeed the whole idea of justice, act as a check and balance to ensure protection for individuals. Rights would be redundant in a society where everything was done fairly to the satisfaction of all.

Hence 'natural rights' and 'natural law' are not found in nature, but are the result of nature being interpreted by human reason. So, for example, the most basic feature of a 'natural law' approach to ethics is that everyone has the right to self-defence – because clearly, defending your life is a basic function of all living things, and it would be unnatural to expect someone not to act to preserve themselves. But that is a rational interpretation – to say that everyone, when threatened, actually defends him or herself, is no more than an observation (and, of course, it may not always be true), but to say that everyone has a *right* to do so is quite a different thing – it is offering a reasoned justification for what happens.

Bentham famously called natural rights 'Nonsense upon Stilts', and argued that rights were not 'natural' but were established by the human subject by consent and agreement. In a natural state (as he observed in 'savage' nations) there is no security, no laws and no government.

His argument goes like this:

• That which does not exist, cannot be destroyed and does not need protection.
• Natural rights do not exist, therefore it is nonsense to set them out and claim to defend them.

He was therefore against anything which defined a basic right that an individual could claim simply by virtue of being born. As far as Bentham was concerned, the only basis for rights was that of 'general utility'. Hence, for him, man-made law and rights go together – you have rights because the law determines them. But where there is no law, as in the state of nature, you can therefore have no rights.

This has led to a criticism of Bentham's utilitarian position, on the grounds that it offers no absolute or final point of reference, no basic requirement that human beings should be treated in certain ways simply by virtue of being human.

Comment

In many ways, this is rather like the argument that there is no morality in the process of natural selection. If nature progresses through a struggle to survive, and species dominate and consume one another in that struggle, it is strange to claim that any one species might have a 'natural right' not to be killed and eaten by another. Rights come about simply because humankind has (Bentham would say for the purpose of utility) devised laws, and from them has given rights.

However, there are those who argue forcefully for natural rights. John Finnis (b. 1940), Professor of Law at University College, Oxford, argues that there are basic 'goods' that have intrinsic value, including life itself, knowledge, friendship and religion. People may think that some of these 'goods' are more important for them than others, but they cannot logically be measured against one another; all are valuable and none should be ignored. His main work on this is *Natural Law and Natural Rights* (Clarendon Press, 1979) which sets out to examine those rights that are required by practical reasonableness and which can be delivered through the law.

But this, of course, follows the general 'natural law' approach that reason can understand and interpret the fundamental, essential nature of reality. To be human implies certain things, quite apart from any subsequent legal agreements.

Starting with rights

Two years after John Rawls published his *Theory of Justice,* another Harvard academic, Robert Nozick (1938–2002), produced *Anarchy, State and Utopia* (1974), which took a very different view of the starting point for justice.

Nozick's argument took as its starting point the Kantian view that people should always be treated as ends in themselves and not as a means to an end. Hence, while Rawls's idea of justice as fairness suggested that it might be right to redistribute wealth in order to benefit the least well off in society, Nozick is concerned to defend each person's rights, including the right to hold property.

He argued that, even if everyone were given an equal share of goods, they would soon start trading and some would end up with more than others. So it is necessary to look at justice in terms of an on-going historical process. People have acquired what he terms 'holdings' and they are free to trade these as they wish, but such trading is based on *consent*. He objects to any attempt to undermine that basic right to property, and views taxation for the purpose of redistribution as a form of slavery – since it attacks the rights and holdings of individual people (making them, in effect, a 'means' to the end of a politically devised idea of a just society).

The task of the state, therefore, is simply to protect individuals and their property. What they do with themselves and their possessions is up to them, not up to the state.

This is a basic libertarian position, and Nozick was to moderate his views in later works, but it remains a powerful argument in defence of rights, and a reminder that the rights of individuals should not become the result of a negotiation or sharing on utilitarian grounds, but should be protected as their basic requirement.

Richard Dworkin (see particularly *Taking Rights Seriously*, 1977) argued that a right should not be something that a person can exercise only if it is to everyone else's benefit, or justified on a utilitarian basis, but is something that can be claimed *even in the most difficult of circumstances*.

In other words, a right is something that, in order to protect myself, I can *insist* on. Whereas in a democracy there is always the danger that the majority inevitably wins out over the minority, the introduction of rights means that individuals and groups can be protected.

A note on tolerance

You tolerate a different point of view if you *disagree* with it, but accept that the other person has a *right* to hold it. A tolerant society is one that accepts the fundamental legal and political rights of individuals. It may not be a harmonious society, or a 'fair' one, but it is one where basic rights are respected.

To take the opposite extreme, the Soviet Union under Stalin was intolerant. People were spied upon, and any word or gesture that suggested a view other than that sanctioned by the Government was severely punished. The aim of that kind of society is to maintain uniformity and compliance. The aim of a tolerant society is to enable variety, discussion and disagreement, without people's basic rights to life, freedom or property being under threat.

- The issue to consider is whether you should tolerate the expression of views that are themselves intolerant.

The 1970s is not universally regarded as the most exciting or inventive of decades, but it certainly was in terms of political philosophy. Notice the dates of significant publications mentioned in this section: Rawls, 1972; Nozick, 1974; Dworkin, 1977; Finnis, 1979. These and others generated a whole new interest in political philosophy.

Recognition

Isaiah Berlin pointed out that, when it comes to the individual within society, a sense of recognition is important. People need to feel that they count for something, and that their views are being taken into account. Hence, people will sometimes put up with a considerable amount of repression if it is done by their own class, or within a democratic structure. They are more likely to rebel, or at least harbour a sense of grievance, if it is imposed by an individual or a group who claims superiority.

People sometimes demand rights, not because they will immediately want to exercise them, or because they are presently prevented from doing something they want to do, but because they feel that those rights acknowledge their place within society. Hence stability and respect for law are likely to be promoted in a situation where the authority to rule, or to make law, is acknowledged by the people, rather than imposed on them. So the key question is how people establish and justify political authority.

Political authority

In *Leviathan* (1651), Hobbes clearly saw the danger of a lawless state where everyone was out for him/herself. Without security, there would be little scope for commerce or co-operative activity, and life would slide into a state of chaos and end up 'nasty, brutish and short'. He therefore wanted people to accept the authority of a ruler, and to commit to accept that authority even if they themselves had played no part in setting it up.

His views need to be taken in context of the English Civil War. When a king who claimed the divine right to rule is beheaded, and when a commonwealth is set up only to be replaced by a restored monarchy, society is constantly threatened by change and uncertainty, and bloodshed was the result of a clash of strongly held views about the nature of authority. Hobbes insisted on strong government. But others, including Locke, wanted to ensure that people had control over the government, rather than have an unchallengeable government imposed on them.

Hobbes believed that once a government is established in a single person or a single assembly, all have to accept the authority of that ruler. Without that, Hobbes felt, there could be no guarantee of security. All have to give up their individual will on the condition that all others give up theirs as well, and thus all are equal in trusting the government that has been established.

However, Hobbes had a single 'get out' clause, and that was that one could refuse to accept the authority of a ruler in any case where one's life was threatened – a crucial and fundamental 'right'.

By contrast, Locke established the principle that government should be held to account by the people. Locke sees people as using the government as an *agent* of their own authority. Governments do what we want; if not, we replace them. The American Declaration of Independence made it clear (following principles set down by Locke) that a government derives its just powers from the consent of the governed, and that people have a right to dismiss that government and set up another. And, of course, that was the point of the Declaration, since the former colonies were complaining about and therefore breaking away from the rule of the King of England.

And, of course, it was Locke's 'agency' approach to government that became the norm for justifying democracies.

Authority *v.* power

Power represents the ability to do something, whether what is done is right or wrong. Of course, some might argue that might is right, and that the power to do something is therefore sufficient reason to do it. On the other hand, it is more widely believed that, if you have the power to do something, the question remains as to whether it is right to do it. That question is one of authority – *authority represents an agreement that the power may be exercised*.

In a democracy, those in power need to be authorized by the people. A policeman may have power, represented by any weapons he carries, but he also needs authority if he is to act – for the authority lies in the agreement that those who are trained and qualified to act as police, expressed often by wearing a particular uniform, are to be obeyed in certain, pre-determined circumstances. Thus, a member of the police, whether on of off duty, whether armed or not, would not, for example, have authority to request sexual favours from a passer by! Their authority is defined and limited, but it also gives them the right to do things (for example, lock a person up) which would be illegal if done by a citizen who was not a member of the police.

Those who have authority but little power must persuade, if they are to be obeyed. Some might argue that the United Nations comes under that category. Individual states, especially if they are powerful, can simply ignore UN resolutions. The bluff is called on authority if it lacks visible and effective power.

Almost everything we do is regulated in some way. We drive on a chosen side of the road, pay taxes in order to have healthcare, education and other services provided for us. We are obliged to behave in ways that are agreed as acceptable, and will be arrested and jailed if we disobey basic rules about private property, or the right to life.

We submit to the authority of the state in almost all areas of our lives – but should we do so?

- What are the advantages to us as individuals from obeying authority?
- If we think that a rule is wrong, do we have the right (or, indeed, the obligation) to protest against it or disobey it?
- Should society legislate as much as possible in order to provide all we might need, and have maximum order? Or should we aim at a minimal society, allowing individuals to decide as much as possible for themselves, and legislating only when absolutely necessary?

For Locke, every individual is required to accept the majority decision, since this is the only way to get unified action, and because the government is given authority by people to act on their behalf. In the same way, people, through their social contract, agree that the government has a right to impose taxes and so on. But again, there is a limit to this. Locke holds that one should not be obliged to accept any situation where there is a direct threat to one's life or property – the same reservation made by Hobbes.

But here there is a fundamental problem. *How can society be stable if individuals have the right to reject their chosen rulers every time their own particular position is threatened by an action taken on behalf of a majority?*

You appoint someone to act on your behalf. If that person is an accountant or a lawyer, you will use them only as far as they put your own wishes into effect. In politics, the appointment of the agent is done in favour of a majority; therefore there will always be a minority who are subject to a government that does not reflect their wishes.

Likewise, there are always going to be situations, even in a democracy, where taxes or laws or restrictions of freedom are going to be imposed on people against their will. The fact that a majority has agreed that this or that politician or government is going to act on its behalf does not detract from the consequent frustration of the minority.

It was, of course, exactly this problem of dealing with minorities that was a weakness of the utilitarian approach to political life. There needs to be some agreement on fairness or on basic rights that does not depend on a utilitarian assessment of the greatest benefit to the greatest number – otherwise, minorities lose out every time.

But at what point should you rebel against a government or a particular law? For Hobbes, it is the point at which your life is threatened. For Locke that same threat extends to your property. But that might be used to justify rebellion on the grounds of punitive taxation. Is that reasonable?

It may also be fairly argued that, in a democracy, where public opinion can change a government, the rights of free speech and free association allow people to demonstrate and make their objections known. Hence, the more rights that people can exercise, the more possible it becomes for them to engage with and influence the political process.

Despotism legitimized?

Even the most liberal of philosophers may sometimes regard despotism as a legitimate form of government, if those to be governed are not capable of engaging effectively in the political process. In Chapter 06 on freedom, we saw that Mill claimed that: 'Despotism is a legitimate mode of government in dealing with barbarians, provided the end be their improvement, and the means justified by actually effecting that end.'

- Would Plato have agreed with this? Do rulers always know best? And do they have a moral obligation to patronize and control people if they consider it to be for their own benefit?
- Does this validate the decision of a ruler to impose a state of emergency or martial law, if the people are seen as 'out of control' in some way?

Anarchy

The logical alternative to the acceptance of political authority is anarchy – the view that each individual should be autonomous and self-governing, and that it is wrong and unnecessary to set up an external authority to control individuals in society. In other words, anarchy is the view that people should be left to organize their lives in their own way.

It can be argued that anarchy can work within small communities, where everyone knows everyone else, because informal agreements can be made between members in order to organize how to get things done. The only sanction for someone who did not fit in with those informal agreements would be exclusion from the community or, at the very least, the disapproval of his or her fellow members. For anarchists, such organization is *interpersonal*, and works from the bottom up, rather than the more usual political authority which is imposed from above by an already established government.

Comment: Housemates rule?

Perhaps, in evaluating whether 'communitarian anarchy' – in other words, rules being established within small face-to-face groups – could work, one might reflect on the popular TV series 'Big Brother'. Clearly, what we witness here are the sorts of tensions and alliances that form when a small number of people are separated off from the rest of the population and put into a confined space.

The whole idea is to see who is best able to thrive in that situation. Some will become unpopular, some popular. Some will try to guard their independence of the group, others will be better at assessing and working alongside other people.

But, looking at 'Big Brother', one might well ask whether anarchists are naïve in assuming that rule could come from the bottom up or, indeed, whether Hobbes was right in arguing that everyone needs strong political leadership.

So, anarchy can be seen in either a positive or a negative way. Positively, it is the view that left to their own devices, people are quite capable of co-operating with one another for mutual support, without the need for imposed rules. Negatively, it is used to describe a situation in which, without rules, it is everyone for themselves – exactly the sort of chaos that Hobbes wanted to avoid.

Rules for family life

Should parents be allowed to smack their children? Is that a matter for legislation or common sense? At what point does the desire of government to make sure that children are protected become intrusive on what is usually regarded as a personal and private matter?

Should you be told when to eat, or how often to have sex? Should parents be required to get their teenage offspring to bed at a predetermined hour, on the grounds that they should not crawl to school next morning having spent half the night playing computer games or using chat rooms?

Many would argue that a family is exactly the right environment for positive anarchy. Some parents might feel that a more negative sense of anarchy, or even a Hobbsian vision of chaos, might result if they did not 'lay down the law' to their offspring.

Anarchy is not just another term for chaos, it is a serious view and worthy of discussion. Almost everyone approves of some measure of anarchy, particularly in matters of sex. If you argue that what consenting adults do in private should remain outside the sphere of legislation, you are – to use the term correctly – in favour of 'anarchy' in the bedroom!

Time and acceptance

David Hume (in *A Treatise of Human Nature* (1740), Book III, Part ii, Section viii) commented on the British monarchy:

> Tho' the accession of the Prince of Orange to the throne might at first give occasion to many disputes, and his title be contested, it ought not now to appear doubtful, but must have acquir'd a sufficient authority from those three princes, who have succeeded him upon the same title. Nothing is more usual, tho' nothing may, at first sight, appear more unreasonable, than this way of thinking. Princes often seem to acquire a right from their successors, as well as from their ancestors; and a king, who during his lifetime might justly be deem'd an usurper, will be regarded by posterity as a lawful prince ...

In other words, once a political system is established and demonstrates that it works effectively, that fact alone will give it a measure of legitimacy. The same is true of laws. What may be seen as an illegitimate infringement of personal freedom when first introduced, may later become accepted as a practical and commonsense measure. The compulsory wearing of seatbelts in vehicles, the requirement for vehicles to pass an annual test of roadworthiness, having to wear a crash helmet on a motorbike and not smoking in public places all limit personal freedom, but all are widely accepted.

Hence, theoretical arguments about how political authority may be justified are never going to be the whole story, since they overlook the pragmatic and the historical aspects. People do not come to power in a vacuum; they do so in a matrix of historical and political currents many of which they do not themselves control. A theory about the authority of a state may serve as a way of justifying a political system, but that does not mean that it reflects the basis on which that authority is *actually* accepted – that may be a far more mundane matter of what people have grown accustomed to, and what seems to work well for them.

Hypothetical contracts

Ronald Dworkin and others have argued that a hypothetical contract is actually no contract at all. It says only what *might* have been agreed, not what has actually been agreed. Hence it may indeed offer a basis for ethical arguments (in other words, it can show what would be fair) but it does not reflect the real situation. In reality, people are born into a political system and are not in a position to opt in or out of any theoretical contract upon which it claims to be based.

As Hume and others pointed out, in considering the earlier tradition of social contracts, people are born into a particular nation; they do not choose to join it. What may feel like justice to someone who actually sits down and negotiates, may feel like an imposition to those who subsequently find themselves living under that political or legal regime.

Therefore we should be very cautious about hypothetical contracts or 'thought experiments'; they are wonderful for sorting out the logic of an argument, or for clarifying basic values, but they do not, and cannot reflect what really happens in the ongoing historical process.

Legislation

What is the nature of law? How far can the law accurately put into effect the wishes of a ruler or government? The philosophy of law is a whole subject in itself, as is jurisprudence, and so we cannot start to examine exactly how the law operates. What we do need to do, however, is see how the operation of the law fits into the general requirement that a political system should promote justice, fairness, equality and freedom.

Plato wrote *Statesman* and *Laws* towards the end of his life, and he seems to have grown rather more pragmatic in his political thought, compared with the earlier *The Republic*. On the one hand, he wants to restrict citizenship in order to exclude those who are incapable of making progress in knowledge and virtue (and thus less able to participate in government), but on the other hand he recognizes that those who are less than philosophers may achieve positions of power. He therefore recognizes that no system is perfect.

Although, in *Statesman*, Plato approves of the process of making and implementing laws, he sees them as *blunt instruments* compared with the sensitivity of a skilled philosophical ruler. This is because laws are inherently unable to see the subtleties and differences that distinguish one situation from another.

In other words, *law is a matter of compromise*. It cannot express, in each and every case, what a wise person would want to see as the outcome.

Example

There are occasions when, in order to end intolerable suffering, a person may – out of love – help another to die. This is murder, since 'murder' is the term used for the deliberate taking of innocent human life. On the other hand any law dealing with murder will need to be applied very sensitively in this case, since the intention is quite different from that of someone who kills a bank clerk in the course of a robbery. Every situation may have its mitigating circumstances.

The crucial issue, if the law is going to be seen as just, is the sensitivity and flexibility with which it is applied. But even in case law, where the record of judicial decisions helps to guide the application of the law, it is never possible to take *all* the particularities of the present situation into account.

In *Laws*, Plato contrasts people's desires (which pull them one way and then another) with reason, and it is the latter which should provide the common law of the state. He recognizes that every society will develop customs, some of which can be applied to everyone and may therefore become laws, and that *reason* (as embodied in the wise ruler) has the role of evaluating different customs and promoting some to the status of law, with the intention that they should then be applied to everyone.

This, of course, leaves open the question of how laws may be framed in a multicultural society. If there is a range of cultural customs, their assessment by reason might not be straightforward, for some will be more important to their particular social group than others. The task of reason, then, is to act as a universal adjudicator between conflicting social customs.

The French Declaration of 1789 described Law as 'the expression of the general will' (a term that is found in Rousseau – see page 51) and goes on to say that every citizen has a right, through his representative, to have a say in its foundation.

But it is important that the judiciary should be properly established and independent of external pressure. In the American Declaration of Independence, the complaint against the King was that 'He has obstructed the Administration of Justice by refusing his Assent to Laws for establishing Judiciary Powers' and 'He has made Judges dependent on his Will alone for the tenure of their offices, and the amount and payment of their salaries.'

Honesty in court?

In his day, as Mill observed in *On Liberty*, atheists were not permitted to give evidence in a court of law – an argument that suggested that unless you believed in a future life (and therefore punishment) you could not be trusted to tell the truth under oath. But he points out that this argument is suicidal:

> Under pretence that atheists must be liars, it admits the testimony of all atheists who are willing to lie, and rejects only those who brave the obloquy of publicly confessing a detested creed rather than affirm a falsehood.

- An oath in court does not guarantee the truth. It simply demonstrates that a liar is aware of the legal consequences of doing so.

Hence, the importance of separating out the three different functions of the state:

- The Legislative body/parliament – frames the laws and establishes the principles upon which the country is to be run.
- The Executive – puts those principles into action, taking as its authority the decisions of the Legislature.
- The Judiciary – puts into practice the laws that have been put forward and agreed by the government.

The important principle is that, if the law is to be applied fairly, it must be independent of the power of the executive, and must not be influenced by any other authority or money.

Branson gives £100,000 to help defend the McCanns

Following the disappearance of four-year-old Madeleine McCann while on holiday in Portugal in May 2007, suspicion eventually fell on her parents, Gerry and Kate, when no convincing leads to either find an abductor or her body were forthcoming.

In September, Sir Richard Branson announced that he would be giving £100,000 to launch a fighting fund to help in their defence. Convinced of their innocence, he wanted to provide the means for them to get access to the best legal help in preparing their case.

- What does this say about the law?
- Should innocence be more easily proved for those able to fund the best legal advice?
- Is it right to provide funds for a defence in a case that could lead to a criminal prosecution? If so, might those not so fortunate as to have the cash claim that the outcome of their own cases were adversely affected?

At the same time, a YouGov poll for The *Sunday Times* showed that 48 per cent of those interviewed thought the McCanns could have been involved with their daughter's death (although this included the possibility that the death was an accident).

- Is it right that opinion polls of this sort should be taken and published?
- Is it possible for someone to receive a fair trial if public opinion, based on whatever information is given in the media, is strongly for or against the innocence of the accused?

How much law do we need?

Both Plato and Aristotle thought that the purpose of law was to help people live better, offering summary guidance based on the wisdom of the rulers. But does more legislation automatically lead to a better quality of life, by giving additional guidance, or does it unfairly constrain the individual? What areas of life should be free of law?

In *On Liberty*, Mill says:

> No person ought to be punished simply for being drunk; but a soldier or a policeman should be punished for being drunk on duty. Whenever, in short, there is a

definite damage, or a definite risk of damage, either to an individual or to the public, the case is taken out of the province of liberty, and placed in that of morality or law.

Clearly, this follows his general, utilitarian approach to freedom and morality. Private matters should not require legislation. He is also against the sensitivities of any religious or cultural group being legally imposed on others. He gives two examples of this:

- Since Muslims, through the tradition of their religion, do not eat pork, he argued that within Muslim countries eating pork can be made illegal. But if it were made *universally* illegal, that would be wrong.
- The Puritans in New England – or in England during the time of the Commonwealth – forbade most forms of entertainment. This, he thinks, is wrong because it is the imposition on the whole of society of the sensitivities of a minority. He was therefore against the imposition of Sabbath restrictions on entertainment and work.

The two maxims Mill applies are:

... that an individual is not accountable to society for his actions, in so far as these concern the interests of no person but himself.

... that for such actions as are prejudicial to the interests of others, the individual is accountable, and may be subjected either to social or to legal punishment, if society is of the opinion that the one or the other is requisite for its protection.

Hence, for Mill, the justification for punishment is essentially a matter of social protection. There are at least five reasons for punishment:

- retribution
- deterrence
- protection of the public
- rehabilitation and reform of the law-breaker
- vindication of the law.

All but the first of these is in the general interests of society, and may be justified on a utilitarian basis. From the perspective of political philosophy, the last is important, because it suggests that if the law is seen to be broken with impunity it will no longer command respect, and will therefore fail to perform its basic social function. The first, retribution, is very different, in that it assumes that some actions are such that they deserve to be punished, quite apart from any subsequent benefit that the punishment might achieve.

One might want to ask whether retribution, taken in isolation from the other four, is ever sufficient reason for punishment, but that takes us into a whole range of questions of a broadly ethical character, rather than being specific to political philosophy.

In terms of rights and justice, the main thing to recognize here is that the law is an expression of the authority of the government. The issue of whether it is ever right to protest against or break a law, is therefore equivalent to asking when it might be right to protest against or seek to change a government. Locke held that the government was accountable to the people. Logically, the law, too, must be so accountable. A law that does not have the broad consent of the people may be enforced, but without consent it is difficult to see how it could be described as just.

The proof of the pudding ...

David Hume is a philosopher who can generally be relied upon for sharp observation and common sense. He argued (in 'Of Civil Liberty', one of his *Essays Moral and Political*, 1741) that monarchies had improved recently, since they were:

> found susceptible of order, method, and constancy, to a surprising degree. Property is there secure, industry encouraged, the arts flourish, and the prince lives secure among his subjects, like a father among his children.

This is his straightforward way of judging the effectiveness of a political regime – that it leads to security and human flourishing. That seems to be a fair way to assess whether or not rights, justice and the law are well applied.

That remains true in the twenty-first century. To say that a country is democratic simply means that its leaders are elected; it does not imply that its people are free or that life is stable and civilized. Both Afghanistan and Iraq, for example, have elected governments, but that does not stop chaos and bloodshed. President Mugabe is an elected head of state in Zimbabwe, but that does not guarantee fairness or equality for its people. The key to a stable and civilized life for any nation is the application of a benign rule of law; 'benign' because the imposition of draconian legal restrictions by a military junta, for example, does little to secure the long-term co-operation of its people. Where the law is perceived to be fair, it is most likely to be obeyed. That in turn leads to respect for government and political stability.

Of course, the more cynical may follow the observations of Nietzsche in Part 2 of *On the Genealogy of Morals* (1887), who argued that people rationalize their obedience to the law, and think that they are being moral, but in fact they obey first and foremost because they have no alternative. Politics, however much 'social contract' theorists might like to think it based on reason and consent, is actually based on *power* – an argument that goes right back again to Thrasymachus in Plato's *The Republic*, and the argument that justice is whatever is in the interest of the strongest.

08

gender and culture

In this chapter you will learn:
- about the battle for gender equality and representation
- to consider whether there should be positive gender discrimination
- about the issues raised by multiculturalism
- about the role of religion in society.

We have already seen that the broadly liberal agenda in political philosophy has focused on freedom, equality and the autonomy of individuals. But at the same time, there has been criticism of the central place given to the individual in this agenda. Conservatives like Burke (see page 64) or Oakeshott (1901–90) argued that more attention should be paid to the social traditions and views that, passing from generation to generation, build up an accumulation of wisdom. Communitarians pointed out that people do not act as isolated individuals, but what they do is related closely to their place within society. Oakeshott himself argued that people are not abstract rational selves (in the way Kant conceived them to be, in his ideal 'kingdom of ends' where everyone is an autonomous individual), but are real and embedded in particular circumstances. Hence, politics cannot simply be a matter of applying abstract rules, but rather 'attending to the arrangements of a society'.

In terms of ethics, F. H. Bradley (1846–1924) argued that, in deciding what was right, one should take into account the various responsibilities one had within family and society – in other words, that one place in society brought with it certain duties, and moral dilemmas occurred when different social duties conflicted with one another.

And that divide between the emphasis on the individual and on society, runs deep within philosophy:

- On the one side you have the rationalist and idealist tradition of philosophers such as Descartes or Kant, along with utilitarians such as Bentham and Mill, and in more recent times, existentialists like Sartre, who all look at the individual with his or her choices and dilemmas, and then explore their social implications.

- On the other you have Hegel and Marx on the socialist side, along with conservatives like Burke, who start with society with its traditions and its ongoing process of change. For this tradition, people are who they are because of the place they have in society; it makes no sense to abstract them from their community.

And that divide lay behind the discussions in the 1970s initiated by Rawls's idea of the 'original position', where he considered what people would choose to do if they were behind a thick veil of ignorance about their place in society. His critics pointed out the impossibility of such ignorance – we know who we are, because we know the place we have within our family, society, nation and so on.

So how does this impact on gender and culture?

From the liberal side, a good starting point might be the United Nations Declaration of Human Rights (1948). Article 2 states:

> Everyone is entitled to all the rights and freedoms set out in this Declaration, without distinction of any kind, such as race, colour, sex, language, religion, political or other opinion, national or social origin, property, birth or other status.

On the other hand, surely your experience of life, your social needs, opportunities and aspirations are going to be very different, depending on all these factors: your gender, race, social origin and religion may do more than anything else to define who you are. Is it realistic that politics and law should take none of them into account?

We shall therefore look at issues of gender, and then at the particular problems posed by multiculturalism.

The essence of womankind

For the most part, until the twentieth century, philosophy was dominated by men, and represented a particularly male view of the world. Feminists have sought to counter this by arguing:

- that women should be treated on an equal basis with men
- that the distinctive role of women in society should be recognized and appreciated.

The first of these is aligned with the liberal tradition, the second with a more communitarian approach.

But first we need to ask whether womankind has a distinctive essence, different from that of the males of the species. If that is the case, then it might provide an objective starting point from which to argue for a particular relationship between the sexes.

Plato considered that women were capable of becoming Guardians, and therefore that they were capable of becoming educated in the same way as men (*The Republic,* Book 5). He thought that natural abilities were equally distributed between men and women, but that women remained the weaker sex and should therefore be given duties lighter than those for men.

However, the equal opportunities for men and women came at a price, for he wanted selective breeding – pretending that the right to have children was allocated by lot, but actually selecting only the most athletic men and women – and he removed his potential Guardians from family life, intending that those who did not know their own parents would treat all those of an appropriate age with equal parental respect. Men and women are equal, but only by isolating them from the normal influences and role-models that might produce gender differences.

Aristotle, however, held that women were unable to reason well (or effectively), and that they were therefore better suited to be ruled. He did not see this as in any way against the interests of women, but argued that since they could not rule themselves they should welcome the help given them by men. He saw women as too much ruled by their emotions, and therefore needing the rational guidance of men, who were better suited to command.

Notice that Aristotle argues on the basis of his view of the **natural essence** of women, to justify a system in which men took responsibility for political decision-making. He was not the only one …

Kant claimed that 'the philosophy of women is not to reason but to feel' and that, in a marriage, the couple would be guided by the knowledge of the man and the taste of the woman. In other words, while accepting that the sexes could work well together, he sees their essence as quite different.

Rousseau made a virtue out of Kant's necessity, and considered that women should not be taught to reason. He argued that women were able to use their emotions to manipulate men, and feared that, if they were also taught to reason, they would have undue power over men.

In one of his clearest statements, in his book *Emile*, he declared that the role of a woman was to make herself attractive and to be subject to man, with her strength chiefly in her charms, by which she is able to arouse men to action. Although endowed with boundless passions, a woman is given modesty to restrain them. She shows her power through the profession of weakness. Men find that their pleasures depend on the goodwill of the female sex, and are therefore taught to offer them their attentions, in the hope of reward. In the end, the man is enslaved by the woman.

Rousseau's comments are frequently of a covert sexual nature and should not always qualify as rational philosophy – as when he claims that, in their moral relations, a man needs power and will, while the woman's need is merely to offer little resistance! But his general argument is clear: he wants women to be educated to accept, willingly and cheerfully, a position subordinate to that of men.

Nietzsche, in comparing what he saw as the 'slave morality' and 'master morality' (see page 75), feared that women would be more prone to accept the slave moralities of the weak, and Sartre, in *Being and Nothingness*, saw women as more open to anxiety and despair and therefore more likely to fall into what he termed 'bad faith'.

Are women essentially different from men? That is the question that lies behind all these views. If they are different, is that difference such as to alter their place in society or their political rights or duties?

And given the way in which – from both social contract and utilitarian standpoints – people agree together on the basis of their needs and wishes, the key question becomes:

• Are men and women equally capable of directing themselves, thinking effectively and developing their own life-plans and values?

If that is the case, then the logic of the social contract, and all the arguments in favour of equality and justice, should require the elimination of any sexual discrimination.

However, that is only one side of the issue. It shows that women and men are equal when it comes to participation in the political processes that men have established. But do those political processes recognize the distinctive nature of women's contribution and insight? In other words, it is one thing to establish parity with men, another to make sure that the political agenda is balanced between the concerns and values of men and of women.

Women and freedom

Mary Wollstonecraft (1759–97), whose *A Vindication of the Rights of Women*, 1792, was published the same year as Thomas Paine's *The Rights of Man*, argued that men and women were equal on the basis of intellect, and was angry that men had assumed that they should be controlled by propriety, and restricted by prejudices. She was concerned particularly with education, believing that to be a major factor in preventing women from fulfilling themselves in society and working alongside men as equals. She boldly attacked and undermined the view of women presented by Rousseau:

> Women are ... made slaves to their persons, and must render them alluring that man may lend them his reason to guide their tottering steps aright. Or should they be ambitious, they must govern their tyrants by sinister tricks, for without rights there cannot be any incumbent duties.

(From *A Vindication of the Rights of Women*)

In other words she acknowledges and mocks what Rousseau saw as natural. She argues that a woman's first duty is to herself as a rational creature and as a mother. She makes the point that women are held back even from developing their own personal qualities, asking 'how can a being be generous who has nothing of its own? or virtuous, who is not free?' Wollstonecraft herself found intellectual stimulus by being a member of a group of thinkers which included Thomas Paine and, later, William Wordsworth. Her book should be seen against the background of radical political debate triggered by the revolution in France – ensuring that the rights of women, and their particular needs, were not neglected in the broader campaign for political rights.

Probably the best-known work to argue for women's equality, prior to the twentieth century, was J. S. Mill's *The Subjection of Women*, 1869. He was of the opinion:

> That the principle which regulates the existing social relations between the two sexes – the legal subordination of one sex to the other – is wrong in itself, and now one of the chief hindrances to human improvement; and that it ought to be replaced by a principle of perfect equality, admitting no power or privilege to the one side, nor disability to the other.

His campaign had an ideal precedent – the recent abolition of slavery in the United States. He argued that, prior to its abolition, many people had argued that black people could not govern themselves, and therefore that slavery was entirely natural for them. The same argument had been used against women, and he now set out to refute it, and to argue that men and women should be treated equally.

He did not argue that women should be given any special treatment, simply that prejudices should be removed, and the law of supply and demand should determine their work and contribution.

> What women by nature cannot do, it is quite superfluous to forbid them from doing. What they can do, but not so well as the men who are their competitors, competition suffices to exclude them from; since nobody asks for protective duties and bounties in favour of women; it is only asked that the present bounties and protective duties in favour of men should be recalled. If women have a greater natural inclination for some things than for others, there is no need of laws or social inculcation to make the majority of them do the former in preference to the latter. Whatever women's services are most wanted for, the free play of competition will hold out the strongest inducements to them to undertake.

Here we have the voice of a utilitarian and free-market economist. Indeed, he argues that until women have been given a chance to explore the range of their natural abilities, society will not know the benefits they have to offer. To the accusation that women have more nervous energy and emotion than men, he points out that if their energy were more channelled in business, for example, it would be less likely to show itself in changes of mood.

He claims that there is a great waste of mental talent by not allowing women the freedom to do all that men are able to do – not totally wasted, since domestic arrangements etc. are of value, but limited in a way that then sets them apart from men. Hence, allowing men and women equal access, the pool of talent available in any sphere would increase.

In the end, it comes down to prejudice. Mill argues that:

> ... the generality of the male sex cannot yet tolerate the idea of living with an equal. Were it not for that, I think that almost every one, in the existing state of opinion in politics and political economy, would admit that injustice of excluding half the human race from the greater number of lucrative occupations, and from almost all high social functions; ordaining from their birth either that they are not, and cannot by any possibility become, fit for employments which are legally open to the stupidest and basest of the other sex, or else that however fit they may

be, those employments shall be interdicted to them, in order to be preserved for the inclusive benefit of males.

Negative and positive freedom for women

In Chapter 06 we noted the distinction between positive and negative freedom. Notice that with Mill you have a natural progression from the one to the other. It is not simply a matter of removing restrictions that society places on women, for example, the gaining of the vote or legislation that requires equal treatment in the workplace, but of looking at the positive freedom that women now expect to shape their lives as they wish. In other words, it is not enough to claim that women are free to do things on an equal par with men, unless society offers such possibilities equally. It is one thing to be free to do something, another to be able to do it. Freedom *from* prejudice allows freedom *to* develop.

Moving forward to the mid-twentieth century, another major work about the place of women in society is *The Second Sex,* 1949, by Simone de Beauvoir (1908–96). Her book explores the various myths about women and the roles they are expected to perform for the benefit of men – that of wife, lover, mother. In particular, she argues that women are not born to the roles that they end up adopting, but they accept them because that is what society expects.

She sums this up in her famous line 'One is not born, but rather becomes a woman.' Clearly, there is nothing natural about the position of women in society; it is (rather literally) man-made.

And here we touch on a feature that will come up again when we look at multiculturalism and post-modernism – that the political agenda is not based on some absolute or 'natural law' approach, but is simply the product of a choice to follow one or more social constructs. Society is as it is because that is what we choose it to be; it could be quite different. There is nothing inevitable about the place of women; they are not born to particular roles. There is nothing in the essence of womankind that holds her back from exploring her positive freedom.

Women and representation

Today, we take it for granted that a key feature of a successful democracy is adequate representation. In other words, if the political process is to reflect the wishes of the people, then the interests of all should be taken into account, both in terms of access to those who are elected to represent them, and in the selection of representatives in the first place.

It is worth pausing, therefore, to remember that women only received the right to vote in Britain in 1918, and even then it was restricted to women over the age of 30, who 'occupied premises of a yearly value of not less than £5'. It was not until 1928 that the voting age for women was brought into line with that of men.

The question now is not whether women have the right to vote, but whether the present system of elections provides sufficient representation for them within Parliament and government. Is the fact that there are more men than women in the British House of Commons simply a feature of social assumptions and opportunities which favour men?

Positive discrimination

In an ideal representative democracy, every group would be fairly represented in the decision-making process. The result should be that the general views of society and law would reflect the interests of all alike.

However, that is not always the case, and there are situations, for example, in employment law or the selection of candidates for election, where particular social groups feel that they are unjustly excluded or face particular obstacles in achieving parity with others.

In such cases, it may be argued that the balance should be restored by introducing positive discrimination. In other words, if all other things are equal, a decision should be made in favour of that representative of a group that feels it is unfairly treated. This can apply to women applying for work, for example, or members of a racial or religious group.

However, there may be problems with positive discrimination:

- The person appointed may not be accepted by his or her peers as having gained the position on the basis of his or her merits.
- There may be resentment on behalf of those who believe that they are better qualified but now being discriminated against in favour of those who now receive positive discrimination!

In an ideal situation, no discrimination of any sort would be practised, and therefore no positive discrimination would be needed. In such a situation, Mill's market-forces argument might work – that people would only do what they are best qualified to do. But even if that were put into practice fairly, it might still result in women not receiving the same treatment as men. Issues today include equal pay, or the 'glass ceiling' beyond which women do not seem to go in terms of promotion within a company.

The dilemma is whether market forces or positive discrimination are the best, long-term answer to remaining grievances. Those feminists who take a Marxist analysis argue that capitalism is inherently unfair on women and that men and women can only be treated equally when other social distinctions are also set aside. Today, with the dominance of capitalism and liberal democracy globally, the free-market (with minor social adjustments to promote equality) seems to be the most favoured approach.

Gender and distinctiveness

Even if women and men are treated by law as equal, it can be argued that their contribution to society is different from that of men. Particular qualities (for example, sensitivity, compassion, nurturing, skill in the bringing up of the young), may be displayed by both men and women, but are traditionally thought of as feminine. Clearly, society as a whole benefits from a balance of 'masculine' and 'feminine' qualities, by whichever gender they are displayed, but how is that best achieved? Should gender differences be celebrated or minimized?

Carol Gilligan (*In a Different Voice*, 1982) showed that 11-year-old boys and girls think quite differently about moral issues. Presented with the same dilemma, the girl considered mainly the relationships involved, while the boy treated the same dilemma rather more like a mathematical problem, weighing up the options.

And today it remains broadly true that there is sexual stereotyping in the toys children are given and the style in which they are dressed. For all that gender equality is accepted in terms of the law, the right to own property, the political process and the workplace, gender distinctiveness is proclaimed from every advertisement.

In the western media and advertising world, sex is still used to sell products, whether they are designed to appeal to men or women. This contrasts with the rather coy approach, and blatantly sexist rules of 50 years ago.

Oxford hoax girl named

> The name of the girl undergraduate of St Hilda's College, Oxford, who disguised herself as a man and dined in hall at Lincoln College on Saturday, was revealed to the college authorities yesterday.

Thus began an article in *The Daily Telegraph & Morning Post*, 2 December 1953. Both she and the male student who had invited her as a guest into the hall were 'rusticated' – sent home for the remainder of the term. The article described how she returned to her home near Aylesbury 'wearing a corsage of carnations given to her by an undergraduate before she left'.

Her mother commented 'I don't wonder Felicity was taken for a boy. I saw her on the river last term. She was wearing slacks, and from a distance I could not tell the difference.'

- Notice the assumptions of 50 years ago. There was no hint that it was wrong of the college to allow only male guests. Nor is the idea of dressing as a boy in order to go against that rule seen as anything other than a foolish prank. But the reporter could not help but insert the comment about the corsage – a nice feminine touch.
- Whatever rules and restrictions may have applied in the past, they need to be seen against the background of the general views and assumptions of the day.

One reason why feminism has a rather different angle on politics, is that is recognizes the importance of family life and interpersonal relationships. Earlier political philosophy tended to focus on the ordering of society and public life, rather than on the more intimate arrangements of marriage and family. However, issues such as the right of a man, on marriage, to take over his wife's property, brought the public and the private together in a way that reduced the freedom of women. Today, it is more difficult to pretend that domestic life is not closely bound up with the social and political – tax, benefits, education, health provision, are all political issues that impact directly on domestic life.

Example

The provision of social welfare, support for single parents and so on, is made on the basis of an evaluation about the relative value of family life and employment. For example, a government may try to encourage mothers to return to the workplace, rather than remain at home with their children. This, whether right or wrong, suggests that becoming part of the conventional workforce is more important that childrearing, and that it is therefore going to be more rewarding economically to return to work. If the values were different, it might be argued that women should be paid to remain home with children, rather than find work outside the home.

At the same time, there is the issue of whether men and women are being treated equally when it comes to home and family responsibilities. Or whether men and women are treated equally in employment, if they are of an age when they might be expected to have a family.

In other words, there is a general recognition that one cannot separate the political from the domestic – the one automatically impacts on the other.

The 'enlightenment' view, reflected in liberal politics and utilitarianism, sees people as individual, autonomous human beings, of equal status and requiring equal freedoms and rights. Clearly, at the time when these principles were first established, women were not given equal rights, and have therefore had to fight for their equality.

But that is only half the story. In the great sweep of political philosophy, there have been two very different strands of thinking. One of these, typified by Kant, tries to establish rational and universal principles that can then be applied to everyday situations. The other, typified by Hegel, sees people as always embedded in an historical process – in real, physical communities, and thus open to all the influences of their particular time and place.

The 'enlightenment' project represents the first of these – but it tends to abstract individuals from their particular setting, considering what rights and freedoms I should have *in general*, rather than what rights and freedoms I need in the particular circumstances in which I live. Communitarians counter this by arguing that we are embedded individuals. We are shaped by our families, our communities, our religious or social traditions, our economic circumstances, and by the place where we live.

This applies equally to men and women. Women, for example, have a special role in producing and nurturing children; they have a natural ability to form supportive friendships and they may be members of a religion that has a long tradition of seeing women in particular roles and not in others.

There are, for example, communities in Holland where men and women choose to dress in traditional dress, reflecting their Calvinist religious background. Muslim women may prefer to wear the traditional dress of that tradition. To the 'enlightenment' mind, both appear to be restrictive and indicative of an attitude of repression. The French education system will not permit Muslim girls to wear even a headscarf in school, since they want to emphasize the enlightenment ideal of equality rather than cultural distinctiveness.

It may therefore be argued that women need to be cautious in accepting equality too readily on the basis of the male enlightenment stereotype – of which the power-dressed female executive is perhaps the icon – simply because that may do less than justice to the distinctive social experience of women. Those who are not convinced of the value of this liberal individualism and autonomy may see such women as repeating the mistakes of men.

So the feminist perspective has contributed both a critique of the male-dominated nature of politics (with the demand for equality and for proper representation) and also a demand for a proper recognition of the nature and contribution of women in society, and a consequent shifting of the political agenda to reflect it.

Multiculturalism

Multiculturalism is the view that people should respect and celebrate different cultures. It does not require an ironing out of cultural differences, but encourages mutual understanding. It tends to go hand in hand with the general view that there is, in any case, no single 'correct' answer to any political, philosophical or religious question.

The alternatives to a multicultural society are:

- A society where only one culture is accepted and allowed. Foreigners are tolerated, but are required to conform to the social and cultural norms when in public.

- A society where there is either hidden or open conflict between different racial and cultural groups, or where these groups separate themselves off into ghettos.

Iranian police give barbers the chop to enforce Islamic dress code

Under this heading, an article in the *Guardian* (25 August 2007) described the way in which some barbers were closed down after being accused of being 'purveyors of decadent "western" culture.' Some women's salons had been closed for offering tattoos and some men's barbers closed for providing eye-catching haircuts. This was done as part of a campaign to enforce Iran's Islamic dress code, especially amongst the young. Young men were ordered to have another haircut and then report to a police station to see if the new style was acceptable.

This can happen because Iran follows a single cultural norm; it is an Islamic state. From a western perspective, where multiculturalism is the norm and religious rules are not legally enforced, such actions seem an infringement of the rights of individuals. But from the perspective of Islamic law, a government has a duty to maintain order and respect – and that applies to things that, in the West, would never be considered open to political determination.

- Should the laws of a nation be determined by religious views?
- What of the position in the USA on abortion or embryo research? Are such positions taken on religious grounds?

Multiculturalism tends to create problems for some of the basic arguments and approaches in political philosophy:

- A utilitarian approach tends to favour majorities rather than minorities. Should a racial or cultural group be required to conform to a norm set by the majority, if that is deemed to be in the best interest of the greatest number?
- Rights are assumed to apply to all citizens alike. How do you adjudicate between a right that is given to all citizens and the pressure to conform to the values of a minority group? For example, drinking alcohol or having an abortion (if certain criteria are met) might be legally and socially acceptable within a secular society. But some religious groups would consider both to be immoral. How do you enforce those

rights, without at the same time acting against the values of
that cultural or religious minority?

Honour killings

The most stark example of this clash between a secular 'right' and
a religious and cultural minority is the so-called 'honour killings' of
girls who are thought to have brought shame on their families by
dating men who do not belong to their religion or culture.

Clearly, by law, such killing is murder, and is punished as such.
Within the family or cultural group, however, it may be seen as an
obligation in order to preserve the honour of the family.

In the earlier 'social contract' approach to legitimizing
government, it was assumed that all citizens would be roughly
alike in terms of their perceptions of what life was for, and that
they could therefore agree on common rights and values to be
promoted by their chosen form of government.

The challenge to Rawls's idea of fairness was that people could
not decide how society was to share out its goods from behind
their veil of ignorance, because in the real world people *always
knew* their place in society. We have now seen that this applies
also to gender and cultural differences. Individuals do not exist
as abstract 'citizens', their political views and needs reflect their
family, locality and cultural roots.

Within a multicultural society, one way of dealing with
differences is by a utilitarian weighing of preferences. But that
will always penalize those who are in a minority. The logical
alternative is to ensure that individual rights are respected,
whether they are of those in the majority or the minority. But in
that case, how do you cope with any conflict that arises between
those rights and the established traditions of the minority group?

Multiculturalism tends to imply relativism of values, and this
moves politics in the direction of post-modernism.

Post-modern politics

Post-modernism is a difficult thing to define. In general it is the
view that there is no one essential truth or perception, but that
everything we think or say is the product of a whole range of

images and concepts that we find around us. Post-modern politics suggests that political ideas are not based on any essential quality of humankind or society, but are the product of individual perceptions and images, always relative to a particular situation. A post-modern politician is likely to be more concerned with creating and selling an image to people, rather than working rationally from first principles to decide what is right.

Post-modernism is relativist – everyone uses and combines ideas in their own way, and it is impossible to say that one is right and another wrong, or that one theory is inherently better than another. It is therefore sceptical about any claims to universal truth.

Post-modernism also tends to be anti-rationalist, breaking down the difference between reality and fiction, so that post-modern politicians may use the media and create images and give a particular 'spin' to every piece of news. Post-modern politics is therefore dominated by a global media culture in which opinions are formed and changed.

Post-modernism negates all 'metanarratives'; in other words, it claims that there is no single 'story' that can be told to make sense of the world, no single theory that can explain it (of the sort that Hegel or Marx expounded); there are only optional images to play with and manipulate.

To follow up on this

Philosophers who take this approach include Jacques Derrida, Jean-Francois Lyotard and Michel Foucault. For those who want to explore this branch of philosophy in more detail, there is *Teach Yourself Post-modernism* in this series.

The fundamental issue here is between essentialist ideologies (i.e. those political theories that claim to be based on a rational assessment of human society and its needs) and a post-modern relativism. In a post-modern world, images and lifestyles are traded, but without relationship to fundamental structures. A government is there to present images for the people to buy, others bid with better images. What is lacking is the sense of any absolute good or ideal on which the political process could be built.

Apart from anything else, one effect of post-modernism is to allow politics to dissolve into economics. In the absence of strong ideologies or absolute principles, the perceived value of a government may be based almost entirely on whether it delivers economic benefits for its citizens. There is no single direction for society or source of wisdom; rather, a wide variety of political ideas and value systems are commodified and placed on the open market – not one of which can claim any exclusive justification.

Relativism and religion

Back in 1991, after the fall of the Soviet Union, André Gorz wrote:

> Can a society perpetuate itself without direction or orientation, without any aim or hope? Can it perpetuate itself when the economic performance and efficiency which are its permanent obsession have as their supreme goal an excess of comfort? Will not a growing number of men and women be tempted, then, to seek refuge from this absence of hope and orientation in abstractly religious – if not, indeed, fundamentalist – systems of thought?

> *Capitalism, Socialism, Ecology* (trans. Chris Turner, Verso, 1994), p. 1.

This issue, only then becoming visible on the global horizon, is exactly the one that faces us today. However loudly the liberal democratic tradition and capitalism proclaims its success in delivering the goods and freedoms that people desire, there is still a void that consumerism itself does not seem to satisfy.

That void may be expressed religiously or philosophically, but also in terms of belonging – the desire for a society within which the individual is respected and feels that he or she is able to contribute to some overall goal, and to matter. This is seen in the rise of the fundamentalist and politically radical form of Islam. The basic tenets of Islam – of submission to the fundamental and essential reality called Allah, and the recognition of Muhammad as his prophet – sets up values that are in stark contrast to those of post-modern economics and politics. If that religious absolute is subverted into political radicalism, it provides a motivation for a crusade against what are seen as the intrusive values of capitalism and the individualist ideology embedded in liberal democracy.

The gesture of suicide to demonstrate a cause, is one that acknowledges a value that, for the individual, is beyond that of life itself – sweeping away all the 'goods' offered by liberal democracy.

This sense that there are some absolute truths worth dying for – which is there in most world religions in one form or another – presents an unstoppable opposition to liberal politics, because it rejects the promise of individual benefits that is the latter's *raison d'être*.

Oil and control

In debating the underlying reasons for the 2003 Iraq war, some have suggested that the motivation was the control of oil supplies. Others have pointed to the desire of the USA to steer the Middle East towards democracy, and encourage that part of the world into a free-market capitalist economy. As we shall see later (page 211) this was part of the overall neo-conservative agenda in the USA.

The implication is that the struggle for influence in the Middle East is fundamentally on behalf of the liberal democratic agenda. Far from being the political option of choice for all who are free to choose, it is now opposed by various groups who express fundamentalist religious and political views. Faced with the offer of western relativism, there is a backlash in favour of fundamentalism.

And this, of course, only reflects a similar rise of Christian fundamentalism and moral absolutism in the USA itself (seen particularly in connection with abortion and gay rights) in the face of the perceived threat to traditional values posed by liberal individualism.

Religion is about a rejection of superficial images and lifestyle options, in favour of a quest for what is enduring and essential in life – exactly those things that a post-modern culture rejects.

The danger is that the absolutism of religion can too easily become wedded to the absolutism of a political ideology. Where that happens, liberalism, relativism, individualism and democracy itself may be seen as an enemy to be opposed.

Headscarves and bikinis in Turkey

An article for the *Observer* (6 May 2007) by Peter Beaumont highlighted the clash of symbols that confronts modern Turkey, illustrated by a photograph of women wearing headscarves in front of a huge poster advertising a bikini. There had been demonstrations in Ankara against the perceived threat to the secular state from those who would promote a stricter Islamic lifestyle.

His analysis suggested that an underlying problem is that a wealthy, educated, secular and westernized elite, which has held power, is now feeling threatened by the growing influence of the middle class and urban poor, who are generally more conservative and religiously observant.

Turkey was established as a republic in 1932, and its constitution prevents religious laws from dominating society, separating religion from the state, even though 99 per cent of the population is Muslim.

This may partly account for the resentment of 'America' in some quarters, for it has come to represent a state where any form of traditional order has given way to mobility and market forces, where individuals have to make their own way, and in which all previous cultural and ethnic roots are melting into a single, materialist society that is devoid of higher values. Now this, of course, is not a serious assessment of the United States, but it is an image that has been festering away in the minds of many of those who fear its economic dominance and military power to coerce. It was true for Gorz, writing in 1991, and it remains true today.

Religion in a free society

Put in an historical perspective, freedom to practise religion is a recent phenomenon. Following the Reformation in Europe, nations divided between Protestant and Catholic, frequently persecuting those who did not conform. Before that, the clash between the expanding Islamic empire and old Christendom led to bloodshed. And before that, Christians were intermittently persecuted within the Roman Empire. Forced conversions and intolerance are not the preserve of any one religion.

So a first question might be: *Should religion be excluded from the political arena?*

In the United States, there is freedom of worship, but religion is officially excluded from the state political and educational apparatus. However, that does not prevent issues from arising where state provision seems to cut across religious views. Should creationism be taught alongside natural selection in schools? From a secular point of view, it is clear that the responsibility of the state is to teach whatever is regarded as the established science. However, for those who accept a literal interpretation of the Bible, that secular perspective is taken to be one-sided, and they seek a balance. If fairness is established, either on a utilitarian basis or one of preserving basic human rights, it could be argued that a government should provide what a majority, or even a significant minority want, provided it does not offend others.

Britain has an established religion, while accepting freedom of worship. The issue in this situation is whether other religions should be treated on an equal basis with the established Church. Should denominational schools be funded by the state? Should they be required to teach all religions in an objective way? Should funding for denominational schools be allocated in a way that is proportionate to the membership of each religion?

In any case, if religious observance is measured by those who attend a place of worship on a regular basis, the majority of the British are secular – which would suggest that state funding of religious schools is inappropriate, were it not for the fact that many secular parents opt for their children to go to faith-based schools, on the basis that they may receive education in a more morally sensitive context.

A recent issue in France was the wearing of the Muslim headscarf by girls at state schools. The French approach to religion and culture is that minority groups should comply with the norm of French society and should not be allowed to stand out from others on the basis of cultural or religious identity. Then, as we saw above, in Turkey the issue is whether a secular state is threatened by the strict adherence to a religion of which the vast majority of the population are members.

These different situations suggest that there is no simple political formula for ensuring that religious groups, whether a minority or majority of the population, will be entirely satisfied with the secular arrangements of the state. On the other hand, states that officially base themselves on religion – as for example, those that practise Islamic Shari'a law – are then challenged on the grounds that the secular concepts of human rights and freedoms are curtailed in favour of religious traditions.

Mill on religious toleration

Having argued for freedom of conscience and that nobody should be accountable to anyone else for his or her religious beliefs, he notes:

> Yet so natural to mankind is intolerance in whatever they really care about, that religious freedom has hardly anywhere been practically realised, except where religious indifference, which dislikes to have its peace disturbed by theological quarrels, has added its weight to the scale. In the minds of almost all religious persons, even in the most tolerant countries, the duty of toleration is admitted with tacit reserves.

On Liberty

The problem in any multicultural, multi-faith society is how you square the democratic right to practise any religion or none, with the exclusive claims of individual religions. To prevent someone from making exclusivist claims is to apply exactly the form of rigid, exclusive rules that the multiculturalist wants to avoid. So, in the name of being liberal and fair, one might have to accept the right of others to argue against being liberal and fair!

09
nations, war and terrorism

In this chapter you will learn:
- to consider the role of the nation state
- about what constitutes a just war
- about the political challenge posed by terrorism.

In discussing freedom or fairness, we have tended to think in terms of a single political framework – the sovereign state – within which people can decide how they should be governed. But not everything happens at this level. War and terrorism go beyond its boundaries, minority groups may seek autonomy within a state, and the state itself, as we think of it today, is a fairly recent phenomenon.

States

At the time of writing, 192 sovereign states are members of the United Nations. They range in size from the huge Russian Federation to the compact Vatican City, but they have one thing in common – that they are recognized as autonomous political entities, with their own government and legal system, and internationally accepted boundaries. Within those boundaries, they are 'sovereign' – in other words, they are self-governing, and may rightly object if other states try to interfere, or to invade their physical borders.

But autonomous nation-states, as we know them today, have emerged only during the last 300 years or so. When you go back to the time of the Ancient Greeks, the political unit under discussion was the *polis*, or city-state, then there are kingdoms, empires, local self-governing republics, and areas where there was no single political structure at all. Until the eighteenth century, most of the world outside Europe was controlled by merchant companies, whose trading areas became colonies of whichever European power sponsored them. Australia was a wide open space waiting to be colonized, into which Britain could send convicts. Africa and South America were carved up by European powers – bringing some form of political control into areas being explored for commercial gain. The American colonies were still ruled from Britain until 1783.

And even with the emerging of nationalism in the nineteenth century, there was still great flexibility in the shape of states. Both Germany and Italy were formed out of federations of smaller states. In the Middle East, the former Ottoman Empire was divided up into protectorates and newly formed states (with the later addition of Israel) whose boundaries were negotiated or imposed and therefore inherently unstable. Through until the latter part of the twentieth century, even in Europe, there were changes in the borders and names of states – as happened particularly in the Balkans, with the break up of the former

Yugoslavia. The failure of Soviet Communism in the 1980s profoundly affected the status of the previously satellite soviet states, as they gained independence.

Warfare had always been a feature of competition between kingdoms and empires within Europe, but the rise of nationalism only encouraged inter-state rivalry and competitive pressure for dominance within Europe contributed to two World Wars.

The League of Nations, set up in 1920 after the trauma of World War I, attempted to stabilize Europe, but failed because of the expansionist actions of Germany and Italy – in other words, it lacked the power to authorize compliance with its desired aims. The United Nations was set up in 1945, and one of the key issues for political philosophy is the extent to which it (or any other) international body can have authority over individual states.

Not our subject!

All this is a matter of political geography, rather than political philosophy, but some study of the way in which nations have changed provides a useful corrective to the over-abstract analysis of some philosophical texts. Thus there is little point in using the term 'state' without some idea of the range of states today and how they are run. So dipping into political geography gives a valuable backdrop to philosophical arguments.

Nations and states

So far we have used the terms 'nation' and 'state' rather loosely. They now need to be clarified, and for our purposes this may be simplified as:

- Nation – a physical area, whose inhabitants have a sense of shared history, common territory, language and culture. A nation can become a state, or a state can give rise to a nation.
- State – a sovereign political authority. It may or may not correspond to a nation.

A state may be created spanning different language and cultural groups, as with Belgium, or it may be split, as happened when the former Czechoslovakia became the Czech and Slovak Republics. Patriotism, based on national pride and a sense of history, may be a motive to reform the state. But equally, when smaller political units come together to form a single state, that may give rise to a sense of shared identity and nationhood – as for example with Germany or Italy.

A state has its own form of government and legal system. Once you walk over a border between one state and another, although there may be no physical boundary, your status changes. You are now a foreign national, a visitor, an immigrant, perhaps an asylum seeker. You may have crossed that border for economic reasons or political ones, or perhaps simply because you are on holiday.

The key feature of today's world is mobility. People cross the world for many different purposes. One person may escape from state 'A' to state 'B' because they fear persecution, while another may travel from state 'B' to state 'A' on holiday! At the same time, workers move from one country to another, and companies extend globally.

Nationalism tends to celebrate roots of language, land and culture. In doing so, it is tempting for it to regard those who share those national roots as deserving of a privileged status within the state, compared with immigrants. This tendency has a long and sad history, with the persecution of minorities who, for whatever reason, have found themselves displaced.

The other side of that issue, however, concerns identity. With mobility, there is a breaking down of old connections with a particular place and way of life. Some may sense themselves to be truly cosmopolitan, without any strong link to their national roots. Others, simply because they are removed from their original homeland, may emphasize that national identity and endeavour to preserve their customs and language.

Within a multicultural environment, you may therefore have at least three distinct groups:

- Those whose background links them to the national culture and language.
- Those who have come from elsewhere, but who regard themselves as fully integrated into a cosmopolitan culture, or their adopted national culture.
- Those who have come from elsewhere, but who cherish their original cultural heritage and preserve its language. The 'problem' here is that integration with the rest of those who live in the state may be restricted, and hence they may choose to live in what become cultural ghettos.

The problem, in terms of political philosophy, is how you reconcile the considerable differences that exist between people living within its borders, with the concepts of equality and rights that are implied by the theory of the state. Can everyone be treated alike, and should they be? Political theory may suggest that this is the case, but the historical differences may suggest otherwise.

Examples

Within a sovereign state, there may be minorities who feel that their particular interests are not properly recognized. They may also seek a measure of autonomy for their own community. The Basques within northern Spain, the Kurds within Turkey, Iraq and Iran, and the Tibetans within China would be examples of this. In all these cases, national and cultural roots have given way to the imposition of the boundaries of sovereign states, to the frustration of those who want to preserve their distinctiveness. In the case of China's claim on Tibet, of course, this situation is made more difficult because of Tibet's strong Buddhist religious tradition, conflicting with the secularism of the Chinese rulers.

In 1995, the Dayton Peace Accord ended the civil war between Muslims, Croats and Serbs in Bosnia. The country was divided into two mini-states: the Serb Republic and the Bosnian-Croat Federation. Each had their own parliament, legal system and police, but a Presidency was established over the top of these, in the hope of uniting the two into a single state. But, at the time of writing, there remain deep rivalries between the ethnic groups. Whereas before the war the different groups had lived alongside one another, now they have generally moved into their respective parts of the country, but resentments remain and full integration is opposed, particularly by the Serbs.

- It is realistic to expect political structures to overcome ethnic, cultural and religious differences?

At its worst, this problem manifests itself as 'ethnic cleansing', where whole groups of the population are expelled in order to create a society where the national heritage appears to match the sovereign state.

The invisibility of the state

Nations are visible. They comprise a geographical area, with its people, language, traditions and so on, in so far as they form an identifiable entity. Nations have a long history and may have gone through many political upheavals.

By contrast, states are relatively invisible. A state is a political entity, comprising – in the case of a democracy – a parliament for deciding upon national strategies and laws, an executive for carrying out the business of government, and a judiciary for putting into effect the laws that a parliament has approved. It also comprises those bodies that control security – the police, in terms of internal security, and the armed forces for external security. In some states, of course, the military may take over the functions of parliament and government.

The state is therefore a set of political structures and power relations, agreed (or imposed) on the people of a nation, in order to provide the benefits of government and law. States can be changed – both in terms of their status and their boundaries – *because they are artificial constructions, not chunks of land.*

Example

With the fall of the Austro-Hungarian Empire, the state of Czechoslovakia was created in 1918. This was invaded by Germany during World War II and then occupied by the Red Army. In 1946, the Communist party came to power, and Czechoslovakia was a communist state until 1989 when a peaceful protest led the Communist party to relinquish power. In 1993, the country was divided into two states – the Czech Republic and the Slovak Republic.

The details of all this, although fascinating, need not detain us. The point here is that a single country or nation can go through political changes (some peaceful, some due to war) that fundamentally alter the nature of the state.

Hence the major divide between the conservative and liberal points of view. A liberal, recognizing the essential artificial nature of the state, wants to emphasize the right of individuals to shape their own destiny and to enter into social contracts and so on. A conservative, conscious of long-established traditions and customs, wants to emphasize continuity.

What should the state do?

> Government, even in its best state, is but a necessary evil;
> in its worst state, an intolerable one.
>
> Thomas Paine, *Common Sense*, 1776

Aristotle's aspiration was that the state could and should encourage people to live well. At the other extreme, Paine saw it as a 'necessary evil' – a view taken up by political anarchists. Part of the task of political philosophy is to try to arrive at a view of exactly how much government can and should do. Some see it as crucial in protecting human rights and controlling the negative aspects of human behaviour. Others see society as well able to take care of itself, and wish government simply to provide the minimum political structure within which freedom can operate.

Whatever the state does, it does with money raised through taxes. In 2004, the utilitarian philosopher Peter Singer wrote about the ethics of President Bush (in *The President of Good and Evil: Taking George W. Bush Seriously*), and commented on one of his comments on taxation, that 'It's your money!' which Singer calls 'folk libertarianism'. Bush, of course, takes the view that what a person earns is his or her own money, and taxes should therefore be kept to a minimum.

The problem with this, as Singer is quick to point out, is that we only earn money because we are part of a social and economic structure. Without society, money has no value: What can you do with banknotes, if nobody recognizes their value? Hence, the paying of tax may be seen as contributing to the maintenance of the society that enables you to earn money in the first place.

But the fundamental issue raised here is really about the *amount* that the state should do – since the more it gathers in tax the more it is able to do by way of social provision and so on.

Thomas Hobbes argued that the sovereign had four duties:

1 To defend the nation against foreign enemies.
2 To preserve peace and internal security.
3 To allow subjects to enrich themselves.
4 To allow 'harmless liberty' (i.e. freedom that does not threaten security).

The assumption here is that people do not want to be involved politically. What they really care about is their economic welfare, and once they are secure from threats both external and internal, what they want is the freedom to increase their wealth. Provided it does not endanger security, that is what they are left to do. This is the starting point for what might be described as a 'minimalist' view of the work of the state.

Go for the minimum

In 'On Anarchy', a section from the second part of his *Rights of Man*, Thomas Paine says:

> The more perfect civilization is, the less occasion has it for government, because the more does it regulate its own affairs, and govern itself; but so contrary is the practice of old government to the reason of the case, that the expenses of them increase in the proportion they ought to diminish. It is but few general laws that civilized life requires, and those of such common usefulness, that whether they are enforced by the forms of government or not, the effect will be nearly the same.

This view, although generally modified to recognize a greater degree of control than the early anarchists would have wished, is still popular. Some philosophers, including Robert Nozick, opt for a fairly minimal role for the state – providing external defence and internal law and order, and beyond that leaving its citizens as free as possible to see to their own affairs.

This approach, which is broadly *liberal*, is concerned to allow individuals maximum control of their own lives. Health and education should be the responsibility of individuals, banding together to organize health insurance and to pay for schools. By way of concession, a minimum is provided to ensure that the poorest receive some help, but as an ideal, the poor should be encouraged to work to improve their situation and no longer have to rely on state aid.

This is the opposite of the broadly *socialist* approach, where the state takes responsibility for the welfare of its citizens, and taxes everyone to a level sufficient to cover the costs. The argument here is that provision of planned services is fairer and more effective than leaving everything to the open market, with the minimum of safety nets. On the other hand, the problem here is that – as with the totally planned economy of the Communist state – universal provision too often leads to inefficiency, bureaucracy and lack of accountability. By and large, enterprises motivated by profit and directly accountable to and paid for by customers tend to be more efficient than those which are centrally managed.

The economy

The amount that the state does, determines its level of taxation, and therefore also its intimate relationship to the economy. In a political system where individuals expect the government to facilitate their own wishes in terms of life opportunities and provisions, governments are judged by whether or not they deliver the goods. This leads to questions about whether a government should become involved with economic and banking decisions, or whether that should be left entirely to market forces, whatever the potential social outcome.

Bank alarm for Labour

In the light of the intervention of the Bank of England to support the troubled Northern Rock building society, adversely affected by the crisis in global inter-bank lending, the *Sunday Times* commented in its comment column (16 Sept 2007):

> The criticism of Mr Brown will be that he presided over the excesses that are now unwinding in the money markets and the economy. New Labour was so keen to establish its pro-enterprise credentials that even obvious excesses and injustices went uncriticized ... He and his ministers have also failed to distinguish between encouraging free markets, which is good, and irresponsible market behaviour, which is not. Old Labour used to prop up coalmines, steel mills and shipyards. Under new Labour, a mortgage bank that offered 125% loans and increased its lending by 55% this year is propped up by a taxpayers' loan. Truly a story for our times.

- The key question here is the degree to which it is right for governments to intervene in the economic decisions of banks and companies.
- How is a balance to be struck between free-market economics and a utilitarian concern that the welfare of the whole of society should not be threatened by it?

Internal security

Few would disagree with Hobbes that the state has a duty to defend itself from both external threats and internal disorder. However, a crucial question here is the degree of control and surveillance that is required to maintain that security, and whether there is a point at which the rights and freedoms of individuals are put at risk. To what extent, for example, are people prepared to have their activities monitored?

Surveillance facts about Britain

- There are 4.2 million CCTV cameras (one for every 16 people), making Britain the most-watched nation.
- About 3.6 million DNA samples are held, including those of 140,000 innocent people.
- In the 15 months to March 2006, there were 439,000 requests for communications traffic data (i.e. requests for legal bugging) of which 2243 were approved.

(Source: *Independent*, 21 August 2007)

Guardian of lifestyle and morals

How far should governments be involved in determining the lifestyle and environmental concerns of their citizens?

Treasury leak

In the autumn of 2007, a leaked Treasury paper came to light suggesting what the British Chancellor of the Exchequer might do in his 2008 Budget concerning the most and least polluting cars. The draft proposal was that an extra purchase tax should be levied on the most polluting cars and 4 × 4s, and that a rebate should be given to those buying the smallest and least polluting. In this way, economic decisions encourage (without compelling) people to take a more environmentally-friendly option.

In this situation, freedom remains (you can still pay up and do what you want) but the government attempts, through its financial management of the economy, to influence personal decisions. The same applies, of course, to taxes on tobacco products and so on.

Should governments take this line, and on what basis is it made? Clearly, if it is in the interest of the majority that there is less pollution, then such a move can be justified on utilitarian grounds (the greatest benefit for the greatest number) – with individuals given incentives to do that which is to the general benefit. This suggests that governments have a moral role to play – just as parents or guardians might encourage children into good habits by the use of incentives.

Similarly, governments can provide safety nets for those who are foolish and get themselves into economic difficulties, or who deliberately act in ways that cause them physical harm. Drug addicts are given medical treatment, even though their abuse of substances was their own choice. Equally, financial help is available for those who either cannot work, or who regularly fail at their jobs. Unemployment pay and social security payments are a safety net.

But is it right for government to act in this way? If its sole task is to organize the economy and defence of the state, both internal and external, then there is a case to be made for absolutely minimal involvement in the personal lives of its citizens. A minimalist state would leave individuals either to their fate, or to enjoy their profits. This might be the conclusion of the approach taken by Nietzsche – who did not want the healthy to be restrained on behalf of the sick, and therefore criticized both Christianity and democracy.

But such an approach cannot be morally or socially neutral. Those who think they are likely to do well if left to their own devices tend to opt for less regulation; those who struggle to maintain themselves will opt for more intervention and help.

In the end, there is a fundamental decision to be made about the nature and function of government: Do you want a minimalist government, and be free and responsible for sorting out your own life (provided that basic security is provided), or do you prefer to live in a society where everyone contributes towards the universal provision of services, and you have the confidence of knowing that, whatever happens, you will be provided for?

Media censorship

By what standards do and should the media operate? Can they ever be totally objective in their reporting? Most papers tend to favour one or other of the main political groups – should that be permitted?

> **'All news must be good news, says Chinese government'**
>
> According to Jonathan Watts, writing in the *Guardian* on 18 August 2007, there had been restrictions imposed on the press, requiring them to report on the positive benefits to the environment of removing more than a million cars from the roads in a four-day trial, but not to report the consequent overcrowding in buses. Equally, press were banned from reporting on the collapse of a bridge in Southern China.

What is more, control of the media is in the hands of a small group of people. They are therefore able to exercise a disproportionate influence over the rest of the people. Is that right, or should a government – chosen, in a democracy, by a majority of the voting public – have authority to make sure that the minority of media controllers are not permitted to exercise an authority above that of the government.

But, of course, without the media, many people do not know what is happening and are therefore unable to make any serious political evaluation – hence a free media would seem a necessary requirement of any democratic society.

Trusting politicians

The issues raised in this section concern the extent to which people should authorize their government to act on their behalf. But embedded within this is another issue – trust. Can you trust politicians to run a state?

Clearly, dictators are generally regarded as a bad thing on the grounds that they act in their own interest, rather than that of the nation as a whole. That is frequently, but not necessarily the case. Although power may tend to corrupt, that remains an observation rather than a logical argument.

But what of elected representatives? Is the operation of government something that should follow the normal moral principles that would guide the relationship between individuals, or is it necessary for a politician to follow an alternative set of values?

Moral politician or political moralist ...

Kant argued (in his essay 'Perpetual Peace') that morality, following the pure practical reason, guides action. It is practical. It leads us to frame a set of laws by which a nation of reasonable, autonomous individuals should be governed (the third of his categorical imperatives). Hence morality is bound up with politics, which determines how the laws that govern a country are framed.

He argues that force is not enough to ensure that all will work together for this common and rational good. Hence we need a moral politician, *'someone who conceives of the principles of political expediency in such a way that they can co-exist with his morality.'* This contrasts with the political moralist who is: *'one who fashions his morality to suit his own advantage as a statesman'*.

And here is a fundamental problem when listening to political arguments that appeal to one's sense of morality. Are the arguments framed in a moral way in order to give strength to an argument that is in fact put forward in order to gain some political advantage? Or are they genuinely moral, and do they therefore determine the goals of the politician who presents them?

In other words, do you trust political/moral arguments, or do you think that, in the end, it all comes down to the control of power?

Machiavelli would argue that the security and defence of the state take priority and may require decisive action, irrespective of the moral sensibilities of the ruler. Kant clearly assumes that his universal moral principles are capable of guiding the politician.

Key questions:

- Do you start with agreed principles of fairness, freedom and rights, and then seek politicians who will make those principles fundamental and shape the governance of the state accordingly?
- Or do you start with the need to maintain a strong and autonomous state, and (if necessary) modify moral principles to fit that situation?
- Plato argued that, for the sake of the stability of the state, people should be told a 'noble lie' about their origins and fixed place in society. Is a government always justified in manipulating the media, if it deems it to be in the nation's best interest?

Sovereignty, identity and representation

Should every nation automatically have the right of self-determination? In other words, should you apply to nations the principles that Mill applied to individuals – that they should be free to do whatever they like so long as no harm is done to others?

Discussions about international relations assume that nations are sovereign – that they should be free from external interference in the way they are governed. This is particularly true of the security of borders.

Turkey and the PKK

The PKK is a Kurdish separatist group, operating within Turkey but with support from within Kurdish groups in northern Iraq. Should the Turkish armed forces be entitled to cross the border into Iraqi territory in pursuit of the PKK fighters or in order to attack their camps?

Both Iraq and the USA argue that Turkey should not do so, but should leave it to the Iraqi forces to deal with them. But what if they cannot do so? The dilemma, of course, is that Turkey does not want to undermine the government of Iraq, and therefore would not – under the normal rules that apply to international disputes – want to cross the border. On the other hand, it perceives the need to deal with the terrorist groups, who are able to inflict casualties on Turkish forces.

On the other hand, if states are always sovereign, does that mean that it is always wrong to violate that sovereignty, if there is reason to believe that the state is likely to become a threat to its neighbours, or is deliberately acting against the welfare of its citizens.

Examples

Although widely condemned, no military action has been taken against the regime in Burma, following its repression of those seeking democracy. Nor has action been taken against, for example, Zimbabwe, in spite of a growing humanitarian crisis in that country.

On the other hand, the USA, UK and others in the 'coalition of the willing' took military action against Iraq on the basis of a belief that it possessed weapons of mass destruction and was therefore a threat. A subsequent justification offered for war was that regime change was in the interests of the Iraqi people.

Does Iran have a sovereign right to develop its own nuclear industry? Does the international community require proof that nuclear material will be used to create weapons to threaten other states, before any military action can be taken to eliminate that threat?

National identity and representation

The government in any representative democracy will depend on securing a majority of those who are elected to represent the people, and one of the important questions in political philosophy is how a government can accurately reflect the wishes of the people. The danger is that minorities, even though substantial, may not have their wishes taken into account if they do not receive a large enough share of the vote to hold a balance of power.

Hence, for example, the Green Party or the UK Independence Party reflect serious but minority points of view. How should those views by taken into account by a government, formed by a mainstream party? Should a party govern by a 'winner takes all' approach to political views and values? If so, how do you prevent radical swings of policy as one party replaces another?

But the issue of representation goes beyond that of political parties. We have already seen that a state is not the same thing as a country or people – it is a political construct. The borders of a state may therefore fail to take into account the various groups who fall within them.

Some nations are put together from different parts of others. Thus, for example, Belgium is the result of fusing together parts of the Netherlands with parts of France. As a result, it is a nation with different languages and cultures; in the north it imperceptibly blends into Holland, as it does into France in the south. There are many other examples of this: in the Balkans, for example, the former Yugoslavia contained within itself many national and cultural differences, which eventually led to warfare and division. Today, the religious and cultural differences between the Sunni, Shia and Kurd populations of Iraq have exacerbated the troubles that have resulted from the American- and British-led invasion of 2003. Nigeria is divided between Muslims and Christians. The partition of India, following its independence, led to huge loss of life when Hindus and Muslims were forced to move one side or other of the borders between India and the newly created Pakistan.

The fundamental question for political philosophy, as we think about these countries is about loyalty, identity and representation. In a country with a single cultural and religious make-up, the citizen may be more or less satisfied with his or her nation, but at least the loyalty is clear. But is one first of all a Kurd or an Iraqi? British or Scottish? Even if the loyalties are compatible, how will they affect the political process? Should I always vote for someone from my own particular sub-group within the nation?

The same is true of religious identity. Is one first of all a Muslim, or a Christian, and only secondarily a British or American national? Does a Sikh have a prime loyalty to the Punjab, home of his or her religion, or to the nation where he or she resides? What is the relationship between the Jewish community and the State of Israel?

In today's multi-faith, multicultural, interlocking world, a religion will comprise people of many different cultures and political persuasions. Equally, any one nation is going to comprise a whole range of people who have loyalties to cultures and religions that extend beyond its borders. There was a time, following the Reformation in Europe, when each nation tended to determine its own religion, and its citizens were required to follow it. That sort of neat division is no longer a practicable option for any country that retains a democratic constitution. You cannot, in practice, achieve a nation with a single religion and culture, without a centralized and authoritarian government which is prepared to impose a religious norm – as, for example, in Saudi Arabia.

So it is even more crucial, in order to achieve political stability, that the democratic process – where it exists – should endeavour to represent each religious or cultural group fairly. But here, of course, we return to one of our fundamental questions. Can that be done fairly on the basis of some *utilitarian assessment of benefits*? In any utilitarian democracy, the wishes of majorities prevail. In extreme situations, minorities rebel.

Minority views and public opinion

It is one thing to think about politics, quite another to be involved with implementing a political agenda. The question is whether, when it comes to the practicalities of ruling a country, people tend to take a pragmatic line, rather than one based on principle. Those in power are regularly challenged to explain why they have proposed some piece of legislation, or have balanced out the needs of different groups of people in a particular way. Does this favour the working people, or the owners of business? Does a particular education system favour people of a particular class, or alienate those of a particular ethnic background?

In answering these, a politician is expected to appeal to fundamental values that he or she shares with those asking the questions. Without some shared values, there would be no meaningful dialogue at all. The politician needs to appeal to basic principles about how those values can be put into effect in society, and it is the strategy for doing exactly that which underpins the manifesto of a political party.

However, public opinion can shift and, if it is not to become out-of-step with the wishes of the voters, a government is going to need to take even minority views into account, since vocal minorities can undermine the credibility of a particular policy. A broad example of this might be the challenging of the assumption that people always and automatically want what will deliver the greatest economic benefit.

The tyranny of money

It is often assumed that the success of a government depends on the ever-increasing living standards of the citizens – and such standards are generally measured in terms of the amount of money and goods that are available to them.

It is therefore assumed that, in terms of political theories, there is no choice but to accept capitalism and a free-market economy, on the grounds that these will provide the best environment for increasing wealth. If everyone is free to make money, untroubled by regulations, then everyone will maximize his or her abilities – and any failure will be down to the individual and not the state.

In such an environment, those who campaign for non-financial benefits may too easily be seen as eccentrics. The economy demands fast and cheap transport; that requires new and bigger roads. To protest about a new motorway scheme in favour of preserving a traditional habitat of a threatened species of butterfly, is regarded as romantic naivety, and it is assumed that the vast majority of the population would prefer the road.

Recently, that has started to change. With the recognition of the threat of global warming, a majority are now coming to the view that it is in the interests of all that the environment in which we live is as important a factor in determining happiness as the amount of money we have in our pockets. This is seen, for example, in the willingness of some people to take lower salaried jobs that happen to be located in a more attractive 'healthy' part of the country.

If money is all, political philosophy becomes but a branch of economics, and political action is determined by the economy. If not, then we are free to re-open all the fundamental questions about how we choose to live and organize our society.

Changing governments

There is a fundamental question that hangs over all political structures. What if they go wrong? What if they fail to meet the aspirations of the people over whom they rule? What if they repress minorities? What if they are seen to be corrupt or self-serving?

In a democracy, voters are able to express their dissatisfaction at the polls, although that, of course, is not guaranteed to bring about the required change. Unless there is an overall majority for one particular party in a majority of constituencies, the result is still going to require a process of negotiation before a government can be appointed that commands a majority of the elected representatives.

But what if that democratic process is not available? What if a government forbids democratic elections for whatever reason? At what point would it then be right to use direct action – or, if necessary, violence – to bring about a change?

History is littered with revolutions of various sorts. Some, like the one that brought about the end of Communist rule in the Czech Republic, are achieved through the sheer weight of public opinion and the size of anti-government demonstrations. Others are achieved only by bloodshed, and many on-going civil wars are simply the long-drawn-out attempt at regime change.

The fundamental question here for political philosophy concerns the justification for taking direct or violent action against a government. Most would argue that this is only justified if all peaceful means have been exhausted. But even then, what right do individuals or groups have to rebel against an established political authority?

One way of evaluating this would be by a utilitarian assessment. How do you assess the benefits to be gained by regime change, against the potential loss of life that might come from the attempt at revolution? And how do you estimate that cost against the continuation of the present government? Thus, for example, one of the debates following the 2003 Iraq war, once the issue of weapons of mass destruction was no longer viable as justification, was the harm done to the Iraqi people by allowing Saddam to continue in power. The problem with the present violence in that country is that, on a utilitarian assessment, it is less obvious that overall people are better off than they were before. *That matter is debatable, but the principle on which the judgement is made is utilitarian.*

The other option is to say that, even if the overthrow of the government might cause more suffering than it prevents, it is still worthwhile to change a government that does not respect certain human rights. In other words, as a matter of principle, certain governments should be opposed, no matter what the cost.

The extreme version of that argument is that of the terrorist who claims that the loss of innocent human life is a necessary and worthwhile price to pay for the possibility of regime change. But that view is generally only taken by those whose views are absolute and fundamental – in other words, it is not the result of some balancing of possibilities, but a campaign in which self-sacrifice is made worthwhile in the greater scheme of things.

The just war theory

It can be argued that warfare and other violent confrontations are not an inevitable feature of international politics, but happen because there is no effective alternative. Here is the view of Hannah Arendt:

> The chief reason warfare is still with us is neither a secret death wish of the human species, nor an irrepressible instinct to aggression, nor, finally and more plausibly, the serious economic and social changes inherent in disarmament, but the simple fact that no substitute for this final arbiter in international affairs has yet appeared on the political scene. Was not Hobbes right when he said: 'Covenants, without the sword, are but words'?

On Violence, Harcourt Brace (1969)

So the first and crucial thing to acknowledge is that war represents failure to secure a rational way of resolving disputes, and can only be justified (if at all) if all possible avenues for peaceful resolution have been explored and are found blocked.

There are two sets of questions to be considered:

- When is it right to go to war? (*jus ad bellum*)
- What rules should apply to the conduct of a war? (*jus in bello*)

The principles of the just war, set out by Thomas Aquinas in the thirteenth century and subsequently developed, are broadly that it may be just to go to war if:

- it is conducted by proper authority. (This is generally taken to imply that war should be carried out by a state, not by an individual or group.)
- there is a valid reason to go to war. (For example, in self-defence if threatened by another state.)
- warfare is a proportional response to whatever had provoked it, and there is a reasonable chance of success. (In other words, massive retaliation as a result of a minor border infringement would be ruled out, as would launching a war when it was clear that little could be achieved by the resulting slaughter.)
- the intention of going to war is to establish peace and justice. (War is not valid as an end in itself.)

Motives for war

I am saddened that it is politically inconvenient to acknowledge what everyone knows: the Iraq war is largely about oil.

Alan Greenspan, former Chairman of the
US Federal Reserve

The key word here is 'largely'. There were other 'reasons' for war: the belief that Saddam had weapons of mass destruction, the need to show strength on the world stage after 9/11. The question must remain whether the economic significance of the Middle East (including, of course, its oil) was a factor in deciding that there should be an enforced regime change in Iraq.

- But are motives for war ever pure?
- Are motives, reasons and subsequent justifications necessarily the same?

The conduct of war is considered right only if:

- it is waged against military personnel, not against civilians. (In other words that the loss of civilian life should minimized.)
- the force used is proportional. (So, for example, a minor border dispute should not be used as an excuse for an all-out military assault.)
- that minimum force is used in order to achieve the war's aim. (This would preclude using weapons of mass destruction, or excessive carpet bombing, if less force could achieve the same military objectives.)

Weapons left by US troops 'used as bait to kill Iraqis'

At a court martial (as reported in *The Independent* on 25 September 2007) the officer in charge of a sniper platoon said:

Basically we would put an item out there and watch it. If someone found the item, picked it up and attempted to leave with the item, we would engage [shoot] the individual as I saw this as a sign they would use the item against the US forces.

This is a clear example of actions that are against the 'just war' and other moral principles. One might consider:

- Killing someone for picking up a weapon, as opposed to directly threatening to use it, seems disproportionate.
- The person picking it up is a civilian, not a member of the military.
- If that were to have taken place in the US rather than in Iraq, it would clearly have been murder, for the possession of a firearm in that country is seen as a right. In Iraq, the possession of a weapon is assumed to be for aggression rather than self-defence.
- Like the invasion of Iraq itself, this is an example of proactive military intervention – not reacting to what has been done, but taking action to avoid what one might reasonably assume will be done.

The two examples given here both concern the Iraq war, since that was in the news at the time of writing. Looking back through history, similar examples could be found in almost all military confrontations. Warfare seldom lives up to the high ideals of the 'just war' theory – but that does not invalidate the attempt to set down principles that should guide the conduct of war, and those who flout them may find themselves on trial as war criminals.

The other responsibility, considered under the 'just war' heading, may be termed *jus post bellum*. This is the responsibility of a victor to ensure that the vanquished nation is made stable and viable. In other words, it would be considered wrong to invade a nation, destroy its military and political structures, and then withdraw to leave its people in chaos. Forced regime change implies a responsibility to establish a viable alternative.

In terms of political philosophy, the fundamental questions are:

- Is it possible to construct a world order in which the danger of war between nations is reduced?
- Is it possible to do so without at the same time having a military capability sufficient to ensure that all nations comply?
- At what point are individual nations likely to tip in favour of abandoning their own military control in favour of an international body?

It is clear, for example in the debate leading up to the 2003 Iraq war, that individual states cannot be forced to comply with the wishes of the United Nations. But does that suggest that the United Nations itself, as a body, should be able to adjudicate between nations and enforce its rules through military action?

The provision and supply of arms is a major worldwide trade, and the supply of arms worldwide ensures that local conflicts are able to continue. In many cases (although not described in those terms) the local combatants act with the implicit approval of those who supply arms. Political regimes therefore depend on those who can supply them with the arms they need for internal or external defence. Thus, for example, the State of Israel is linked closely with that of the USA and the military junta in Burma depends on support from China for much of its trade.

The arms budgets

On 25 August 2007, an article in the *Guardian* (page 21) outlined the defence budgets of Russia, the UK and the USA, in the context of a determination on the part of Russia to revamp its armed forces. The figures quoted in dollars were: Russia: 32 billion; UK: 29.9 billion and USA: 582 billion.

Once those figures are presented, there is almost nothing else that needs to be said in terms of the global balance of power. The USA spends hugely more on military equipment and personnel than any other nation. But it is also worth noting that the figures are considerably lower than at the height of the Cold War. So it is realistic to say that defence costs are in part related to the political situation and perceived threats. It is also true that the Russian investment in defence has increased considerably over the last few years.

In the end, there is a limit to what military force can do in the political arena. It can impose a settlement where there is a dispute, but it cannot guarantee the agreement of all parties to the dispute, nor persuade of the fairness of the result. As David Milliband, the British Foreign Secretary said in the Labour Party conference in September 2007: 'While there are military victories there never is a military solution.'

And, of course, where people feel that they have been unfairly treated, whether as a result of military intervention or exploitation by a dominant trading partner, they may feel powerless to change the existing political or economic structures by legal democratic means, and be driven to take some form of direct action. A sense of injustice lies behind the phenomenon which, while not new, now commands global attention: terrorism.

Terrorism

The attack on New York on 11 September 2001 was, without doubt, instrumental in a major re-think of security, and of the way in which nations can counter the threat of terrorism. There were terrorist attacks before that, including extended campaigns like that of the IRA in Northern Ireland and the Basque separatist movement (ETA) in Spain, but it was the sheer scale and location of 9/11 that made it so significant.

The literature is already extensive, and cannot realistically be reviewed here, but some recent books (for example, Francis Fukuyama's *America at the Crossroads*) have explored and attempted to evaluate the political significance of that event and the resulting 'War on Terror'.

With the rise of the modern nation state, warfare and threats were seen as a state-against-state phenomenon. The scale of the power and weaponry held by states, as opposed to private individuals and groups, made it seem inconceivable that a serious threat could come other than from another state. That is no longer the case. The attacks on 11 September were carried out by an organization that is trans-national. Just as a multi-national company can have branches throughout the world, so it seems an organization that has political or violent ends can be global. This creates a very special problem, for nations are equipped to fight other nations; they are not equipped to fight networks of individuals or small groups.

That was the problem that faced the USA after the attack on New York. It would have been easy if one particular nation could be shown to be responsible – a quick and decisive war might have eliminated the problem. It was not to be so easy, as the wars in Afghanistan and Iraq have shown.

The 'just war' theory is designed to apply to state-on-state violence, rather than terrorism. Clearly, terrorists do not represent any accepted 'authority', nor do they generally, although there are exceptions, respect civilian loss of life. Nor can their actions be deemed proportionate, since it is often unclear what the aim of the terrorist attack is, other than to do damage.

The only principle that might be used to justify terrorism would be the argument that, if one's life and property is threatened, one has the right to defend oneself – a principle set out by both Hobbes and Locke. Terrorism might then be seen as a form of *self-defence* where the imbalance of weapons and power would make a direct military confrontation unrealistic as a way of securing goals. It would also need to show that peaceful means of achieving the terrorists' stated goals had been exhausted. The problem is that, not being a nation state, it is difficult for terrorist groups to enter into bilateral talks in the first place. Government frequently declare that they will not talk to or negotiate with terrorists.

The principles by which a war can be deemed 'just' can also be applied to the military response to terrorism, but here there are considerable problems. A key question:

- Is a nation to be held responsible for a terrorist group that may operate from within its geographical boundaries?

Afghanistan was very clearly a base for al-Qaeda operations, and it was on that basis that the United States went on the offensive in that country, deposing the Taliban regime that had supported the terrorists. But what of Pakistan, which officially opposes such terrorist groups, but is generally thought to have them operating within its territory? What of Britain and other western-European countries? If a terrorist cell based in Britain had carried out at attack in another country, would that justify direct action by the forces of that country on British soil?

The next question concerns the effectiveness of military action:

- Is it possible to defeat terrorist groups through conventional military means?

Simon Jenkins, writing in the *Sunday Times* on 29 April 2007 said:

> Tony Blair claims that the wars in Iraq and Afghanistan are intrinsic to his crusade against terrorism and have made Britain a safer place. Yet both have become confused and bloody occupations of nations whose threat to British national security has been wildly overrated.
>
> The wars have clearly strengthened, not weakened, al-Qaeda and, as far as Britain is concerned, offered a glamorous focus for impressionable young Asians and a training ground for misfits eager for a cause.

And he goes on to suggest that the politics of fear only make the situation worse among Asian Muslims in Britain, whom he describes as 'among Britain's most loyal and motivated immigrants'.

The basis upon which America launched the War on Terror was that of pre-emptive action. It was no longer considered that they should wait to be attacked and then retaliate; rather the US was prepared to take the fight to the enemy. The idea of preventative war was born: where a threat, or potential threat, could be identified, it was deemed appropriate to take whatever action was necessary, including the use of force.

That principle, coupled with evidence (later shown to be incorrect) that Iraq had weapons of mass destruction that were capable of threatening international security, led to the Iraq war of 2003. It was argued that, if Iraq (or any other nation) were to provide weapons of mass destruction to a terrorist group, the results could be catastrophic.

There were two major problems with this:

- A nation, going to war against another nation, can occupy that country and replace its government. However, military action cannot subdue a religious or political ideology. If anything, as has been demonstrated in Iraq, an ideology is *strengthened* when it faces a visible enemy, and it feeds on all the resentment caused by the inevitable casualties of war.
- Because an international terrorist group is based ideologically and not geographically, it cannot be subdued through conventional military conquest. In other words, whatever national target is selected, it is bound to be wrong, and hitting a wrong target always helps the enemy.

There is, of course, another approach. Terrorism thrives on perceived injustice. People join terrorist organizations because they believe there is a cause to be fought for, an injustice deserving of their terror. If the causes of that injustice are removed, then there is less reason for people to resort to terror, and less reason for others to give them shelter or tacit support.

To parody Tony Blair on crime, a balanced moral and philosophical approach to terror might be: 'Tough on terror; tough on the causes of terror.'

Religion and terror

Today it is radicalized Islamic fundamentalists who are seen as the principal terrorist threat. Those who carry out terrorist acts may claim to do so in the name of Islam, but is that correct? The vast majority of Muslims would argue that their faith is one of peace and submission to Allah, and they condemn extremism. On the other hand, Islam does not make a distinction between beliefs and the way of life that expresses them – so Islam is always a social and political phenomenon as well as a religious one.

The debate about the relationship between a religion and acts of terror carried out by its adherents is complex, and beyond what we need to examine here. The key feature is that religion and ethnic or social identity are closely related. Whether it is Christians and Muslims in the Balkans or Nigeria, Hindus and Muslims in India, or Protestant and Catholic Christians in Europe, people have all too often been divided along religious lines, and religious labels have therefore been used to distinguish the sides in the resulting disputes.

The Mountain Meadow Massacre

The 9/11 attack was not the first massacre in the USA to be linked with religion. On 8 September 1857, a party of settlers from Arkansas, travelling by wagon train, were attacked, either by Mormons (who were then a persecuted, minority sect, led by Brigham Young, who had settled in Utah ten years earlier) or Paiute Indians who had been mobilized by the Mormons. The settlers, short of ammunition and recognizing that their situation was hopeless, sued for peace, and a Mormon representative offered them their safety in exchange for their possessions. After they surrendered, both men and women were slaughtered, 140 in all. Only children under the age of ten were spared and sent to live with Mormon families until eventually being repatriated to Arkansas. John Lee, Brigham Young's adopted son, was executed for the crime in 1877. He confessed, but claimed that he was being made a scapegoat.

- Should this historical event colour one's present understanding of the Mormon religion?
- If not, then presumably it is equally right that one's understanding of Islam should not be coloured by the actions of terrorists even if they claim to be acting in its name.

Terrorism and liberty

There is an additional problem with any attempt to counter terrorism. Terrorists, by their very nature, do not abide by the 'just war' principles or the established conventions (for example, the Geneva Convention on the treatment of prisoners). The temptation, therefore, is to counter terrorists by using methods that equally flout those principles and conventions (for example, illegal detention of suspects without trial; torture and inhumane treatment of prisoners; 'special rendition' of prisoners from one country to another for the purposes of torture or imprisonment).

However, a nation retains its credibility and its standing within the international community, to the extent that it maintains the highest standards of integrity in both its domestic and foreign policy. The danger is that by attempting to fight terrorism on its own terms, a nation state is liable, not only to lose the battle on the ground, but also to lose its international standing.

Destroying values

This point was made succinctly by Michael Ignatieff in his Gifford Lectures in Edinburgh in 2003. Recognizing that defeating terrorism requires violence, he asked: 'How can democracies resort to these means without destroying the values for which they stand?'

In the 1790s, Charles James Fox sought to defend individual liberty. He argued that the terror in France did not pose a threat to the situation in England and that the Prime Minister (Pitt the Younger) was wrong to introduce emergency measures.

He claimed that the real danger in such measures was that they give the government power over the individual's thoughts and views.

The situation has not changed greatly since the end of the eighteenth century. Given a threat from global terrorism, the reaction of a government is to place restrictions on people – particularly in terms of surveillance over their actions, and aimed at those groups thought most likely to be involved in terror networks.

The old argument remains – do you take emergency measures to make sure that the country is kept safe (if that were possible), as argued in Britain by Pitt the Younger and by Tony Blair, or do you maintain individual liberty, and take the risk that such liberty will be exploited by terrorists? *It is difficult to see how civil liberties can be defended by suspending civil liberties – that is a constant political problem in dealing with terrorism – on the other hand a pragmatic or utilitarian approach may suggest just that.*

The problem of the nation state, equipped with a military trained in conventional warfare but confronted by the international terrorist network, is perfectly summed up in a conventional saying, quoted by Fukuyama, to the effect that: *When your only tool is a hammer, every problem tends to look like a nail!* That is precisely the problem with seeing a terrorist threat as though it were something that could be sorted by conventional military means.

Terrorists and human rights

Two terror suspects held in Britain but due to be deported to Libya in April 2007, following 18 months' detention, were freed on bail, subject to a 12-hour curfew and a ban on using mobile phones and laptops. This was because two judges ruled that, although it was accepted that people could be sent back to Libya (following an agreement with Libya that torture would not be used on those so returned) the men could be in danger of having their human rights violated if they went back. The Home Secretary had argued that they posed a real threat to security, and that they were members of a terrorist group.

- Which side do you take on this? National security with loss of rights for the suspects, or the maintenance of fundamental human rights, at the risk of further terrorist activity?

Crimes against humanity

Some actions, carried out within a particular jurisdiction and perhaps with the full knowledge and implicit approval of the government, are so horrendous in terms of human life, that they are considered 'crimes against humanity'. The large-scale killing of innocent people or prisoners, for example, would constitute such a crime.

Such acts have been prohibited by international conventions, for example, the Hague conventions of 1899 and 1907, and the Geneva Conventions. These set out how prisoners should be treated and so on. The UN Security Council has also been responsible for setting up various Tribunals for dealing with these crimes, and in 2002 the International Criminal Court was set up in The Hague.

But the problem with any such international body is who is authorized to decide whether a prosecution brought in that court is a valid one, or is politically motivated. The USA, for example, will not allow any case to be brought against American military personnel. The argument used is that a prosecution against an American soldier could be brought for malicious or publicity purposes.

This implies that a nation is in a position to judge the validity of a case that an international body may wish to take up – and hence the international body is placed beneath the nation-state on the scale of authority. Once again, we are up against the issue of the conflict between national and international law. International law is set up by bodies created by the mutual agreement of nation states. Hence, it would appear that the nation states, having established that body (for example, the United Nations) must, in the very act of doing so, agree to accept the authority of that higher body. It is difficult to see how any international body can continue if its authority is open to challenge on a case-by-case basis – whether in the case of criminal prosecutions, or the implementation of resolutions taken by the Security Council.

10 the global perspective

In this chapter you will learn:
- about international relations
- about globalization
- to consider the moral, religious and environmental aspects of global political issues.

Few nations have ever sought to isolate themselves from the rest of the world and even fewer have succeeded in doing so. Trade and conquest have linked nations, formed and destroyed empires, and brought together people from different parts of the world.

It is tempting to think that the global economy is a recent phenomenon, but that is far from the case. In 1848, Marx and Engels published their *Manifesto of the Communist Party*, of which the opening section sets out the impact of the rise of manufacture, trade and the bourgeoisie, and gives the context in which they explain the confrontation between the workers and the owners of capital. Here they describe a phenomenon which is as relevant now as it was in the mid-nineteenth century:

> The bourgeoisie has through its exploitation of the world market given a cosmopolitan character to production and consumption in every country. To the great chagrin of Reactionists, it has drawn from under the feet of industry the national ground on which it stood. All old-established national industries have been destroyed or are daily being destroyed. They are dislodged by new industries, whose introduction becomes a life and death question for all civilized nations, by industries that no longer work up indigenous raw material, but raw material drawn from the remotest zones; industries whose products are consumed, not only at home, but in every quarter of the globe. In place of the old wants, satisfied by the production of the country, we find new wants, requiring for their satisfaction the products of distant lands and climes. In place of the old local and national seclusion and self-sufficiency, we have intercourse in every direction, universal inter-dependence of nations. And as in material, so also in intellectual production. The intellectual creations of individual nations become common property. National one-sidedness and narrow-mindedness become more and more impossible, and from the numerous national and local literatures, there arises a world literature.

Add to this some reference to the impact on global warming of all that shifting of material and goods around the planet, and a hint at the impact of the web on intellectual property issues, and you have an essentially up-to-date comment on globalization!

Perhaps one significant difference today is that neo-liberalism has given birth to the global market, economics is now beyond the control of the single nation, and instant communication means that a crisis in one market will have an immediate impact around the world. Most importantly, information now flows as never before – particularly since the arrival of the internet – cutting across political barriers and allowing individual people to communicate and trade with one another globally. But the trans-national flows of trade, finance and manpower, whereby global trends and forces have become a reality alongside individual nation-states, are a phenomenon that goes back at least until the nineteenth century.

The other aspect of this phenomenon is multiculturalism. A global community means that any one nation-state is likely to become home to people from other continents and cultures. But this is hardly new. People have always travelled for trade or conquest, and found themselves engaging in cultures different from their own – just contemplate the sense of distance from his homeland for Alexander the Great on arriving in India, or a Roman centurion maintaining a distant outpost in what is now Germany or the north of England. Similarly, the problems of holding together a political structure spanning different cultures is certainly as old as the Babylonian empire of the sixth century BCE, whose policy of cultural integration caused the leaders of the conquered Jewish people to find themselves living in Babylon, and struggling to maintain their own identity in the face of the easy option of cultural assimilation with their neighbours. Ancient Babylon was clearly an early example of enforced multiculturalism.

But the crucial difference today is the complexity and scale of globalization. This chapter will simply try to map out some of the main issues that emerge in a global environment.

The international dimension

Global phenomena and issues are those that arise at a level above that of the nation-state – global trade, environment, finance and so on. They impact on individual nations, but are not simply the product of how nations deal with one another.

By contrast, the 'international dimension' of politics is concerned with the ways in which individual nation-states relate to one another and with such bodies that are set up to represent them at a global level. A fundamental question is whether the principles that determine how states interact with one another are adequate to form the basis of a global politics. In other words, are *international* organizations, such as the United Nations, the European Union, NATO and so on, which bring nations together, able to deal effectively with the growth of *trans-national, global* phenomena – like the internet or global money markets?

The other significant thing to keep in mind is that the success of a political system at home is no guarantee that it will succeed in international relations. Ancient Athens may be held up as an example of early democracy in action, but it was constantly involved with disputes with other city-states and with larger confederations of states. By the time of Plato and Aristotle, the real complaint about Athens was that it had failed to keep its empire, and had expended all its strength in its wars with Sparta (the Peloponnesian Wars). So good governance at home is no guarantee of a successful foreign policy.

In looking at the government of an individual state, political philosophy examines various ways by which its authority could be established and justified – the social contract, or a utilitarian assessment of benefits, or the protection of basic human rights, would all count as justification. But how do you establish and justify authority on the international level? And how much authority are individual sovereign states likely to cede to an international body?

The dilemma of authority

Imagine a democracy ruled by a parliament of 192 representatives, who gather to debate and vote on what laws should be applied throughout the state and the principles upon which it should be run. In most democracies, once the laws have been approved, a government and civil service has the task of putting those laws into effect, and it raises taxes in order to do so. Of course, being a democracy, the law is always something of a compromise. The representatives express the views of their own constituencies, but do not always get everything they want – it is a matter of give and take, to achieve the best overall result for the state as a whole.

But in this democracy, things are done differently. Once the laws are decided on, the representatives are sent back home and each has responsibility for implementing the law in his or her own constituency, and to raise funds in that constituency in order to do so. But of course, some will have to return and admit that their own particular view did not prevail in the parliament, and they will therefore have difficulty in persuading their constituents to do what is required.

The situation then gets more complicated, because each of those representatives will want to serve his or her constituents, and will need their support in order to stay in office. Local needs will now compete with the state-wide law and, since each constituency is self-governing in practical terms, there will always be the opportunity to ignore what has been agreed in parliament, or to attempt to delay its implementation.

What is more, the constituencies vary hugely in size. Some feel that they are big enough to ignore the wishes of parliament without any serious consequences. Smaller ones feel that they should not be required to carry the burden of national law, since they have enough trouble running their own constituency.

But since the finance and power is in the hands of the constituencies, it is quite impossible for the central government to overrule their wishes. It can only get compliance by persuading the individual constituencies to accept the agreed laws, and hoping that they will contribute to the cost of implementing them.

Clearly, such a democracy would have little chance of pushing through any radical legislation. In practice, it would always be at the mercy of the larger constituencies, and would have authority only in name.

This is the dilemma that faces the United Nations and any similar international organization. While power remains in the hands of individual members, it does not have the power to enforce its resolutions. Nations can defy it, and it has to negotiate with other members to contribute troops in order to take any action to defuse a crisis. On the other hand, individual states would be reluctant to give up their sovereign status and military power and hand it over to an international body. Apart from anything else, once an international body has power, it is difficult to see how it could be adequately controlled or replaced if it started to act against the interests of members.

Centralized power is therefore unlikely to be achieved. But a central parliament without adequate power, cannot compel, but only persuade, nations to follow its resolutions – and where national interests are at stake, that persuasion may be resisted and the determination to maintain national interests hardened.

Rawls's problem again

A criticism of Rawls's 'original position' thought experiment was that, in the real world, people always knew who they were and where they stood on the social ladder and therefore they could not decide on principles of fairness in a disinterested way. The same is true of the representation of sovereign states on international bodies. Debates and negotiations at the General Assembly or Security Council of the United Nations inevitably reflect the particular interests and alliances of members.

Kant's idea for peace

In 1796, Kant wrote *Perpetual Peace*, in which he tackled the idea of how states could work together.

He saw that the idea of a single global state would not work, not least because of the natural divisions between the people who would comprise it, and the lack of any external body to which to appeal in the event of such a global state becoming tyrannical. Rather, he argued for a federation of states, bound together by agreements to resolve any differences by negotiation rather than by war.

He argued that all the nations who joined such a body should be republican, and that armies should be abolished, so that it would be impossible for one state to attack another. In fact, he wanted an agreement that no state should be able to take over another, or interfere in its internal affairs.

Kant argued that republicanism would be the right form of government if one wanted to achieve perpetual peace, on the grounds that a republic was governed by the people, and they would have most to lose in the case of war breaking out. They would therefore always be less likely to agree to go to war, compared with a monarchy, in which the benefit of the monarch could be seen to override that of the people.

Kant saw clearly that ordinary people had much to gain from a perpetual peace, and therefore had a genuine interest in the international situation, but that this did not imply that they could sit lightly on their commitment to their own nation. Indeed, Kant held that there could be no justification for the overthrow of a state, and that those who attempted to do so should be eliminated as outlaws.

He recognized that an alliance of states would not be easy to achieve, but he thought that international commerce would help it to become a more realistic possibility. In other words, the more reasons there are to bind nations together for their mutual benefit, the more likely that they will also see it as in their interest to set up an alliance for mutual security.

There are two approaches to the prospect of international peace of the sort that Kant aspired to:

- One is that there should be some overall global organization with authority over the individual nation-states that make it up. That is the 'cosmopolitan' approach.
- The other is the formulation of sets of rules governing the relationship between nation-states. In other words, the primary political agency remains with the nations, but they agree (on the basis of enlightened self-interest) to treat each other fairly and in an agreed manner.

An inherent problem with the first of these is that the wide variety of people belonging to that organization would display such different characteristics and aspirations that it would be very difficult to agree on anything – local interests would constantly threaten its stability.

The inherent problem with the second is that it cannot easily become immune from the tendency of more powerful states to opt out of their obligations when it suits them and to try to impose their will on other states.

Sixty per cent of the world's population live within states that are at least nominally democratic. When it comes to the crunch, politicians are voted in by the electors of their own country, and will therefore act in their nation's own self-interest, and their actions are legitimated from time to time by the electorate. Where that self-interest coincides with that of the international community, fine; where it conflicts, tensions arise, and the temptation of any elected politician will be to go with the national rather than with the international interest.

But in an international environment, effective and speedy action would seem to require powers that are already established and agreed. Long-term discussions and resolutions are ineffective in dealing with immediate crises. Hence, the fundamental dilemma at the heart of all international bodies is the conflict between the need for fast and efficient action, and the process of legitimization by consent. Both are needed, but each constrains the other.

Sovereign states

When, if ever, is it right for one sovereign state to interfere in the politics of another?

The theory is that nation-states are sovereign. They control their own destiny, and a key requirement of the state is that it maintains both internal and external security. It has fixed borders and can establish rules about who enters and leaves and it fixes its own taxes and laws.

But states have always interfered with one another, whether by the stick of warfare or economic sanctions or the carrot of preferential trade, the supply of arms, or the provision of personnel to train the military, advise on development and so on.

In general, states claim their sovereignty only when threatened by an unwelcome influence. Thus, for example, whilst recognizing that Turkey had no intention of violating Iraq itself, but only of pursuing the Kurdish PKK fighters who had launched attacks over its border, Iraq still considered that any attempt to cross the border by Turkish troops would constitute a violation of its sovereignty.

Two things need to be considered in terms of when it might be right to violate the sovereignty of a state:

- On what grounds might it be justified?
- On what authority should it be carried out?

The first of these might include the reasons given for a 'just war', in particular self-defence, if threatened by that state. On the other hand, it is then debatable whether a state should be proactive in anticipating and countering a threat, or whether it should only respond once the threat become a reality.

If one state is directly threatening another, the case might seem clear. But would it be justified to invade a sovereign state for the purposes of defending its population against the actions of its government? One could argue, for example, that the rise of the Nazi party and its treatment of the Jews and others, would suggest that the world might have been spared World War II if proactive military action had been taken against Germany earlier. But would that have been justified given the circumstances at the time? Is it seen as justified only with hindsight?

And how do you decide, of all the states that treat their people brutally, which deserve to be invaded in order to spare their own people suffering?

The second of the two fundamental questions touches on the issue of the authority of international organizations. Is the United Nations the only appropriate body to take sanctions against a sovereign state, or it is equally appropriate for that action to be taken by one or more nations acting on their own authority?

'Sons of Buddha' on the march

On 24 September 2007, 100,000 people took to the streets of Rangoon, Burma, protesting against the military regime. Sparked off by a rise in the cost of fuel, but mainly appealing for democracy, the march was led by many thousands of Buddhist monks – thereby giving moral authority to the protests in a country that is mainly Buddhist.

After many days of protests, ever-increasing numbers of troops broke up the demonstrations. Monks were beaten up and many imprisoned and a number of demonstrators were shot. The democracy leader, Aung San Suu Kyi, remains under house arrest (as she has been for 12 of the last 17 years), severely restricted in what she can do. Her Democratic League for Democracy party, with its allies, won Burma's 1990 parliamentary elections, but she was never able to take up her rightful position. Those elections were held just two years after the last major democracy protests, which were brutally repressed.

Of the present situation, the British Prime Minister, Gordon Brown, said: '... there is a golden thread of common humanity that across nations and faiths binds us together and it can light the darkest corners of the world. The message should go out to anyone facing persecution anywhere from Burma to Zimbabwe – human rights are universal and no injustice can last for ever.'

Some questions:

- How can or should the world community respond to the repression of people in a sovereign state?
- Should 'common humanity' provide a basis for military intervention?
- Is the rise of democracy inevitable, and can that justify non-intervention where there is repression?
- What is the difference between this situation and the later justification for the 2003 invasion of Iraq (initially on the basis of a false assessment that Iraq possessed weapons of mass destruction), namely the treatment of the people by the regime of Saddam?

Global networks

Back in the eighteenth century, Adam Smith (1723–90) argued for free-market economics, on the grounds that international trade would benefit everyone. Over 200 years later, international trade and banking and the triumph of free-market economics, as opposed to the directed economies of the old socialist states, is the driving force in globalization. Trade is not the only global network, but it is the one that illustrates most clearly the way in which global influences have come to dominate those of nation-states.

The post-colonial world

Since the 1940s, the old European colonial empires have been in decline, as one by one the major colonies achieved independence. The effect of this was, amongst other things, to open the developing world up to competitive trading agreements, and by the 1980s the dominant view has been that the nations of the developing world would be served best by having free markets within a global economy.

The assumption was that market economics would secure increased standards of living and ensure the former colonies of a place within the world trade system. However, trade is seldom conducted on absolutely equal terms, and the effect of a free market is that fluctuations in the value of commodities – which can be tolerated within a developed economy – have very serious consequences within the developing world, especially where a very large percentage of income comes from a small number of products.

So, in such a world, a fundamental question is whether it is in the interests of developing countries to tie themselves into a global free market, moving from subsistence farming to cash crops, for example, or to accept a lower trade profile and concentrate on subsistence production and self-sufficiency.

Clearly, even where a global free market is the ideal, some regulation and assistance is necessary, leading to the setting up of the World Bank, the International Monetary Fund, the OECD (Organization for Economic Co-operation and Development) and the World Trade Organization. These international bodies both regulate and promote global trade, often by requiring individual states to take action to control their economies, in exchange for support.

But there are key questions here for political philosophy:

The world of global free markets is one *dominated by economics, rather than politics*. But economics is a science, neutral in itself, but relying on political or moral principles in order to express its purpose. It works on Adam Smith's assumption that trade benefits all.

- Is that assumption necessarily correct?
- Is it sufficient as a guide for this new global phenomenon?
- Are there political principles that should dominate economic ones?

Globalization

Globalization refers to the emergence of processes and networks of trade that are not constrained by territorial boundaries. So, for example, the global money markets exist independently of the banks in any one state, and no one state can control them.

Sub-prime chaos!

In 2007, banks in the USA sustained losses in the 'sub-prime' market – the granting of mortgages to people with poor credit records. But those mortgage debts had already been packaged up and sold off to other banks, who thereby shared the risk and the potential benefits. Consequently, as house prices fell and people in the USA defaulted on their loans, the effect was felt worldwide, and banks became more cautious about lending to one another. In Britain, Northern Rock, which had been borrowing on the international money markets in order to fund its mortgage lending, found that its source of money was becoming restricted. As a result it had to apply to the Bank of England for special loans in order to meet its commitments, although it remained solvent. But people, anxious that they might lose their money, queued outside branches of the bank in order to get their cash.

- A single problem – but one which links home ownership in the USA, via a global banking system, to people queuing to secure their cash in Britain. What happens in one part of the world of finance has an immediate effect on all others.
- There was panic, but who was to blame? The sub-prime borrowers who overstretched themselves? The banks in the USA who lent to them? The international system of sharing out

packages of debt? Northern Rock for lending more than it received from savers, and needing to go to the international money market to finance its operation? The Bank of England for not stepping in earlier to stabilize the situation? The media for making a great issue of the problem, and therefore causing people to panic?

Welcome to the globalized world of finance!

The global market means that falls on stock markets in the Far East (reacting to falls on Wall Street at the end of the previous day's trading there) will hit the European markets when they open and, as the sun tracks westwards, will influence the opening of Wall Street for the next day's trading.

Multinational corporations span national boundaries, and operate under different laws in different parts of the world. Employment law and higher standards of living and pay in one place may lead them to shift production to a country where cheap labour will reduce overheads. Products for the market in one part of the world are produced in another.

The global economy also extends to the workforce: jobs are outsourced to countries (for example, India) where there is a large, educated workforce that will accept lower wages, compared with the EU or the USA; manufacturing is switched to China, where goods can be produced for less; practical skills shortages in Western Europe are met by migrants from the countries of Eastern Europe.

Globalization creates a whole new set of issues for political philosophy:

• Nations raise taxes in order to provide benefits for their citizens, but with globalization, people may well officially reside in 'tax havens' where their taxation is lower, even if their income is generated elsewhere. Companies, similarly, make profits for shareholders who reside far from the employees whose work generates them in the first place. Hence we need to consider whether existing concepts of 'fairness' – based on the idea of a social contract within a single state – are adequate. And what does 'fairness' mean for a worker in India who receives a lower wage for the same work as his or her European counterpart?

- If a state finds that its industry is dominated by foreign capital, it is vulnerable to capital outflows in any time of uncertainty. The only way to avoid this is to ensure that its economy is in line with what international capital expects. But once linked into that global network, it is practically impossible for a country to avoid following the principles of the free market. Hence the global economy tends to limit a nation's political choices, and the success of a national economy is now measured in terms of its ability to compete within a global capitalist system.

- Globalization can be seen as a political agent for peace, for if nations are locked together by economic ties, it is unlikely that they would consider themselves sufficiently independent of one another to go to war (as argued by Kant).

Neo-liberalism is the general term used for an approach to economic and political thought that includes the lowering of taxation and economic deregulation. And, of course, with the failure of socialism and rigidly regulated economies, liberal democracy and capitalism became the dominant political and economic options of choice for individual states. Now, however, they have also become the necessary passport to integration into the global economy. *Does that inhibit political freedom?*

Globalization and the law

Trade moves between countries, but law does not. Therefore there needs to be a complex set of regulations to control international trade, otherwise what is acceptable in one place will fall foul of the law in another.

- Under which legal system should multinational companies operate?
- Are multinationals sufficiently accountable to the governments and within the legal systems of any one state?

On an individual level, to what extent should a state be responsible for acts committed by its citizens when they are outside its geographical territory? If someone from Britain commits a crime abroad, should they have a right to be repatriated to serve their sentence, or should they remain in custody within the country in which the crime was committed? And, of course, the severity of punishments varies considerably from one state to another.

- Is that fair? If not, would an internationally agreed system be better, or would that simply undermine the autonomy of individual legal systems?

Being able to trade internationally is important for individual nations and becomes a measure of the success of their governments. Hence the phenomenon of trade being used as a method of furthering political ends, or even to encourage regime change. Imposing economic sanctions is regarded as a more acceptable way of putting pressure on a government than threatening to invade. The more locked into the global market a country becomes, the more it is vulnerable to economic pressures not of its own making.

Turkey imposes sanctions ...

In November 2007, in response to PKK terrorist attacks into its territory, Turkey started to impose economic sanctions on Iraqi Kurdistan, stopping flights between Istanbul and the Kurdish capital Arbil. Iraqi Kurdistan depends on supplies coming through Turkey, so sanctions would bite immediately. A fragile economy needs foreign investment and support, and the threat of sanctions could discourage such investment, thus creating longer-term harm.

But recognition and status are equally important. Hence the phenomenon of states using international events to promote themselves within the global community, and thereby gaining implicit acceptance for their political position. Thus, in discussing countries with a poor record on human rights, for example, one question generally asked is: *Should we be trading with them?* Here there are two options:

- By continuing to trade, nation A hopes to influence nation B, by having its views – as a trading ally – taken more seriously than would be the case if it cut off such links.
- By refusing to trade, nation A hopes to pressure nation B by taking away any potential benefits of that trade and highlighting the unacceptability of nation B's policies within the international community.

As Burma suffers, China must be forced to act

Under this heading, the editorial of the *Observer*, 30 September 2007, commented on the relationship between China and the military dictatorship in Burma in the context of China's international status as host for the Olympic Games:

> China's determination to use the 2008 Olympics to win international kudos gives the world's democracies a rare opportunity to exert influence on Beijing, shaming it into action on human-rights abuses at home and sponsorship of repression abroad.

• Is it right to use an international games event of this sort for political leverage – whether by the host country or by others?

Moral and religious perspectives

Aristotle saw it as the responsibility of rulers to enable people to live the 'good life', and that implied that they should take a moral view of what they were doing. Equally, the 'social contract' approach and utilitarianism both sought to justify forms of government in terms of fairness and protection, which imply a moral view of the nature and purpose of political life.

By contrast, capitalism in itself is amoral – it is about the way trade is financed and whether it is used in a way that a majority would judge to be moral or immoral is a secondary question. Capitalism is about investment and profits; whether these things should be aligned to specific views about the good life, or fairness, or the way people should be treated, is a secondary but important issue.

Globalization is a phenomenon of markets, information and communication. Powered by multinational corporations, it is based on capitalism. Does that imply that it cannot, or should not, have a moral dimension?

But once morality enters into the equation, it is also important to recognize that many people are motivated and guided in their personal lives by religion, and globally religion has shaped different cultures in different ways. It is therefore important to ask to what extent religion is a factor in the global political equation.

The United States is in a curious position now, as the only remaining superpower. While it does not appear to conceive of its efforts as in any way empire building, it sees itself as a custodian for good on the international scene. Convinced that moral right was on their side, the neo-conservatives felt that their nation was in a special and privileged position, and that their foreign policy should reflect that fact.

Moral responsibility

In the 1990s, following the fall of Communism, the neo-conservative view in the United States was that, being the only remaining superpower, the USA had a moral responsibility to use its power for moral purpose. Convinced that moral right was on their side, they believed that the USA could and should use its military and economic weight to change regimes, where that was considered to be in the best interest of global stability or their own people.

Thus, for example, it set about encouraging democracy in the Middle East. The problem, however, is to know to what extent any moral claim remains untainted by self-interest. Was that a genuinely altruistic and moral decision, or was it equally motivated by support for Israel or the need to secure oil supplies? That question is beyond our present purpose. *The key question for political philosophy is whether it is ever right to use military or economic power for a specifically moral purpose and, if it is, how that purpose should be decided and subsequently justified.*

But if politics *is* used for a moral purpose, should that be made public, or should it remain hidden from public scrutiny and another reason for the political action given instead?

This approach has a long pedigree and goes back to Plato's *The Republic*, where he considers it right to put out a 'noble lie' that people are, from birth, destined to be in one or other of the classes within his republic, and that they are therefore unable to chance their fate and place within the hierarchy of the state. Deception, for Plato, is justified in order to maintain order. But if that is practised, then can people ever know whether the reason for which political action is being taken – and on which they might vote in a referendum or election – is the one they have actually been given? And if they do not have that assurance, what is the value of the democratic process to which they subscribe?

This might well lead to the cynical view that political realities are known only to the few, and that the people are fed such information as they need in order to endorse policies that are taken for far more complex reasons than those presented to the public.

Basic question:

- Is the reality of politics different from the issues debated in political philosophy?

I suspect that there are many who have subscribed to this rather sceptical view over the years, including of course Machiavelli, Bentham and Hume, all of whom were determined to reflect on the real political situation rather than an idealized one.

But there are other important moral issues raised by global networks:

Is 'development' a good thing? Is it just colonialism under another guise? On the one hand, it seems right that people should be helped to escape poverty, but on the other there is the danger of poorer nations becoming too dependent on producing cash crops for richer ones, rather than concentrating on subsistence farming and autonomy. Is it necessarily moral to assist a nation to link itself into the globalized market?

What about the movement of people and work? People are less mobile than the economic structures that need them – so it is understandable for businesses to out-source their work to India, rather than employing cheap and educated Indian labour in Britain or the USA. But to what extent does this penalize the opportunities of those in Europe and North America to find suitable work? A huge area for consideration here is the movement of manufacturing jobs to China, India and elsewhere, where overheads and labour costs are less.

- Is that fair to people whose jobs are lost, because they are too expensive?
- Is it fair that, in another part of the world, people work for much less in order to lower the price consumers have to pay for them?

The other side of this issue, of course, is the provision of 'fairtrade' goods – where there is the specific intention of trading in a way that avoids exploiting producers in developing countries. Here the market is shaped by a prior moral commitment.

There are also moral issues raised by immigration. Some sectors of the economy of the USA, for example, depend on immigrant labour, but many of the immigrants entered illegally and remain illegal. They become trapped by a concept of citizenship that is nationally based, while working in a supply-and-demand global economy that is not.

Global inequality

In chapter 05, we looked at the issue of fairness. As set out by Rawls and others, the arguments about what constitutes fairness and how it might be realized in society, were mainly set in the context of a single nation. When we consider the global situation, the issues become far more stark, even if the philosophical arguments remain the same. Without doubt, even if global warming and the terrorist threat are more often in the headlines, the huge disparity in the living standards between the developed and the developing nations present the most pressing moral issue.

- Is it enough to assume that free-market capitalism will eventually spread its benefits to all, thereby eliminating poverty?
- If not, what action, by whom and on what authority, is needed to combat poverty in the developing world?

This is a huge issue, and not one that can be examined adequately here.

The religious dimension

In the wars of religion that followed the Reformation in Europe, the general principle was that each nation, following its ruler, opted to be either Protestant or Catholic. This is an oversimplification, of course, but it makes the point that religion has generally been a transnational phenomenon, even where individual nations have regulated religious practices within their borders.

The 'world religions' are exactly that – belief and value systems that may be followed by people anywhere. They therefore provide people with an alternative way of understanding themselves from that given by the nation-state. In other words, two Buddhists may feel that they have much in common, in terms of their views of life and moral perspectives, even if one lives in Europe and is a British citizen while the other lives in Burma, Sri Lanka or Japan.

The spread of the world religions was therefore a global phenomenon that pre-dated capitalist globalization. They form a layer of self-understanding for people all over the globe that sits over the political or economic.

Where religion and politics are regarded as quite separate – so that religion is regarded as something personal, and as compatible with almost any political allegiance, economic status, or lifestyle – then the religious dimension, however important it may be as a global phenomenon, does not pose a problem for our understanding of global politics.

However, religion is as much a way of life as it is a set of beliefs, and it is therefore liable to clash with any political structures that appear to promote an incompatible set of values. Religions, by and large, hold that certain beliefs and values are absolute, *whereas in a post-modern, globalized world, relativism is the order of the day.*

Hence, the spread of an amoral capitalism, combined with a liberal-democratic view that is generally permissive and relativist, may be seen by some traditional religious groups as threatening to their way of life. This is seen particularly within Islam, where submission to Allah, following traditional Shari'a Law and solidarity with the whole community of Muslims (the Ummah) takes priority over any allegiance to political or social systems. *For a Muslim, the ideal is to live in a Muslim state and under Shari'a law. That implies a political agenda that is fundamentally at odds with the secular ideals of liberal democracy.*

It is therefore not difficult to see how this sense of religious commitment and loyalty, in the face of the apparently unstoppable rise of consumerism, globalization and the relativist values of a free-market view of life, lead some towards radicalized opposition to all these features of the liberal-democratic, globalized world view.

This is not in any way to condone the atrocities carried out by, for example, Al Qaeda and other terrorist groups, but it recognizes that the appeal of such radical Islamicist groups stems from deeply-felt religious opposition to what is seen as an attack on Muslims and the Muslim way of life.

The difficulty faced by moderates, whether within Islam or any other religion, is how to present the moral challenge and the distinctive way of life that their religion teaches, without appearing (to the more fundamentalist and extremist elements) to be compromising with the broadly secular global agenda which threatens those values.

Politics and climate change

However much individuals and individual nation-states can achieve, there are some issues that need to be tackled globally. The threat of climate change is the clearest example of this. In the face of increasing evidence that the accelerating pace of change is in part caused by human action in burning fossil fuels and releasing greenhouse gases into the atmosphere, politicians are faced with an issue which demands that they ask people to change their lifestyle or aspirations in order to achieve something of long-term and universal benefit. Since many political systems are maintained on the basis of enlightened self-interest, this sounds challengingly altruistic.

Eco-war between parties

If everyone agreed that carbon emissions need to be lowered and the environment protected, the question of how this might be done most effectively would be a matter of science and economics. However, within a political landscape, it is thought necessary to claim that things can be changed with minimal pain to the ordinary person – since, in a democracy, it is the ordinary person who, from time to time, is suddenly given political power at election time.

The task politicians tend to set themselves is to make proposals that are likely to be effective in tackling climate change, without upsetting voters.

The fundamental issue, however, is whether one can deal with environmental issues effectively without fundamentally challenging the ever-increasing expectations of consumer-voters. If not, then how are political parties, ever-concerned to maintain their share of the vote, going to present realistic policies?

Without doubt, the answer to the crisis of global warming and other related ecological issues lies within the political sphere. Economics alone cannot solve the problem, because economics is not normative – in other words, it does not decide what *should* be done. But it is equally clear that efforts on the part of individual nations will not be sufficient, since the environmental impact of human life respects no national boundaries, and no one nation is likely to want to take action if others do not, since that might imply a risk to its 'competitiveness' in a global market. Hence the need for global forums to decide what to do and (more difficult) to find a way to give such forums the authority to enforce the changes that are needed.

The Kyoto Treaty

The Kyoto Protocol, agreed in 1997, obliged the industrialized nations to cut their greenhouse gas emissions to five per cent below the 1990 levels by 2012. Some nations have met their targets; others have made no progress at all. Overall, according to a report by two UK-based academics in October 2007, Kyoto had produced no demonstrable reduction in emissions, and it was argued that old-style agreements (which had worked for the reduction in nuclear weapons) did not work, because reduction of greenhouse gases would depend on patterns of human behaviour that affect the whole economy. That will not be changed, just by concentrating on one single feature. They also pointed out that, of the 176 nations signed up to the agreement, 80 per cent of the problem was caused by just 20 of them.

The alternative, of course, is massive investment in new forms of clean energy – but that will be expensive. There are currently 500 projects in its 'Clear Development' project, which gets rich nations to invest in clean technology in developing countries. At the same time, there is the possibility that consumers will become more aware of the issue in their everyday choices, reducing emissions through a bottom-up approach (as presented in an article by Paul Vallely in the *Independent* on 26 October 2007).

There are many questions here, including:

- Which works politically? Top-down imposition of agreements, or bottom-up changes in attitude?
- How does this relate to the issue of individual freedom?
- Is restraint on emissions compatible with a global free market?

International agreements are of key importance, but what level of compulsion can be expected of any such agreement? If a nation does not perceive compliance to be in its own interest, is it likely to accept its recommendations? Clearly, while individual nations can opt out of agreements to reduce carbon emissions, for example, there is little chance that changes that require serious challenges to a way of life or standard of living stand much chance. In democracies, governments stand or fall by their ability to satisfy the people who vote them into power. Only if ecology gets high on the personal agenda of the voters is a government likely to be given the mandate for drastic action.

Establishing the human contribution to climate change was always a key issue in persuading politicians that action needed to be taken. Today there is a general consensus on that point. Whether remedial action will go ahead if it appears to conflict with the needs of business and the drive for higher standards of living, is another matter.

And superimposed on this is the fact that a minority of the world's population consumes the majority of its resources and emits the most carbon.

Fairness

If all were required to cut carbon emissions by the same amount (or even keep them at present levels) it is the poorer nations who would suffer most, simply because the energy required to bring them up to the standard of life enjoyed by the developed nations would inevitably produce more carbon emissions. Hence there is the difficult political task of setting realistic limits to development, as well as to the curbing of the natural capitalist drive towards growth.

This seems to be a re-run of John Rawls' 'original position' debate. Deciding that action should be taken in a way that benefits the least well-off is all very well, but in reality everyone knows who they are and where they stand in the global pecking order. Could fairness ever be agreed, given present disparities?

The problem is that we now have globalization of information and trade. People in developing nations can see and aspire to the level of consumption (and resulting pollution) enjoyed in the wealthiest countries. That sets an aspirational benchmark, and it is difficult to argue that someone who pollutes little should enjoy less by way of goods and services simply to compensate for the additional pollution pumped into the atmosphere by those who are accustomed to enjoy more.

Hence climate change is perhaps the ultimate challenge to political systems. It demands a set of values, power relations, and economic systems that are integrated for universal benefit, rather than the more limited scope of national or personal interests.

It has not been possible, especially in this last chapter, to give any systematic exposition of what philosophers have said on each of these issues – a book could be written on each of the issues, and many have! All that is attempted here is to raise the issues and to give some overview of the crucial questions that need to be addressed.

postscript

What hope humankind?

In October 2007 Al Gore, former Vice-President of the USA, along with The Inter-Governmental Panel on Climate Change (IPCC), were awarded the Nobel Peace Prize for their work on researching and campaigning to make the world more aware of the threats of global warming and the part that human activity contributes to it. Why the Peace prize? Because you cannot separate out issues of peace and conflict from those of sustainable development and ecology. All the issues are now interrelated.

That being the case, we are likely to see an increasingly varied agenda for political philosophy in the future. The days when it was relevant to determine how best an independent sovereign state should conduct its political and economic life are fast diminishing. Business is global, communication is global, the threat of terrorism is global, and now the threat to the environment is global.

Isolationism is a diminishing possibility. States that would like to hide their activities from the outside world are now frustrated by the ability of individuals to use the web and mobile phones to communicate beyond their borders.

Nations may maintain their identity – and so they should, for they carry with them a huge wealth of history and culture. But just as Aristotle recognized that man was basically a political animal, and therefore participation in the life of the *polis* was integral to personal fulfilment, so nations now find their fulfilment by engaging in the global political process.

The debates of 50 years ago are well behind us. No longer do we find capitalist and socialist blocs facing one another. Certainly, in terms of the aspirations of nations globally, liberal democracy and free-market capitalism is the political option of choice. But, as has been shown so clearly by the problems of the 'war on terror' or the assumption that people, once freed from their existing regimes, will automatically opt for liberal democracy, the future is far from certain.

Whether we like it or not, the future of humankind, as a species, depends on finding solutions to political issues. During the Cold War, the main threat was of nuclear holocaust; now the threat is from global warming. And, in addition, there are the on-going clashes of ideology and the inequalities of military and economic power that contribute to social unrest and, at its most extreme, to terrorism. And alongside those, there is the huge disparity in terms of quality of life between the developed and developing nations – an injustice which has not been solved by a global market, and which always has the potential to encourage resentment and with it political instability.

Economics alone cannot solve such problems, nor can science – for both can be used for good or ill, depending on the motives of those who control them. Nor is religion a likely candidate for global harmony, even if each of the major religions may claim to offer that prospect, if only everyone were to follow its path. Each religion comes with cultural and historical baggage which may divide as easily as unite people.

So, in all probability, the future of humankind will depend in large measure on a deepening awareness of the *normative* – of the principles and values which make for the good life, expressed through ethics and thus also through political philosophy.

But that, in turn may well spring from the establishment of a 'normative anthropology' – as advocated by Michael White (see page 10). Unless we establish some common ground for understanding what life is for, some vision of the 'good life' that Aristotle might have recognized, then all politics can do is negotiate between an infinite number of individual human preferences.

Sometimes, there can be agreement on common projects, when the threat to all is clearly defined. On other occasions, one can but stand back in frustration as egos and interests compete. Nowhere is that clearer than in the political arena. Hence the need for political philosophy to stand back from the practicalities of the political process, the power struggles and the ideological battles, and constantly re-examine the fundamental ideas and principles that guide the political sphere of life.

glossary

The following is a selection of terms used in this book, gathered here for quick reference. For more information on each of them, please refer to the relevant index entry.

absolutist Used of moral arguments that suggest that it is possible, in theory, to find moral principles that can be applied universally.

altruism The unselfish consideration of others.

amoral An action that, with respect to the person who performs it, is done without reference to any moral system.

anarchy Used of the view that society would benefit from an absence of law, allowing each individual to be self-regulating.

capitalism The economic system under which goods and services may be traded for profit in a generally competitive environment, and individuals or organizations own the means of production.

categorical imperative An absolute obligation, independent of anticipated results, that forms the basis of moral action. In Kant's philosophy, it denotes that an action is right only if one could wish the principle upon which one acts to become a universal law, and that persons should be treated as ends, never simply as means.

communism Used of the political view that property and the means of production should be under common ownership, overthrowing the class system and capitalism, with each giving as able and receiving according to need.

communitarian Describes the view that political reality is always embedded within a community, rather than a theory applying to individuals.

conservatism Used of a political view that places emphasis on established traditions and values.

contractualism The view that social and political entities originate in, or are justified with reference to, contractual agreements between the parties involved.

democracy Used of a political system in which political authority is established by the people, using a voting system, either directly (in small organizations, or in ancient city-states) or through elected representatives (in modern representative democracies).

determinism Philosophical view to the effect that every act is totally conditional and therefore that agents are not free.

emotivism The ethical theory that moral assertions are in fact the expression of emotions (i.e. to say something is wrong means that you dislike it).

empiricism The theory that all knowledge is based on sense experience.

epistemology The theory of knowledge.

eudaimonia Greek term for 'living well' in a broad sense of both comfortable living and living in accordance with moral principles. It is sometimes loosely translated as 'happiness'.

existentialism A philosophy concerned with individual self-understanding and the problems and finite nature of human existence.

fascism A political philosophy that gives the interests of the state priority over those of individual citizens. Fascism thus tends to be both authoritarian and nationalistic, and the term 'fascist' is loosely used to describe either tendency.

forms, theory of Used of Plato's view of the existence of universals, in which particular instances participate.

hedonism The moral view that the quest for happiness is the goal of human life.

humanism A cultural movement, stemming from the rediscovery of the classical works of Greek philosophy and widely influential from the fifteenth to the seventeenth centuries, emphasizing the dignity of humankind and the centrality of human reason as opposed to the unquestioning acceptance of tradition.

ideology The structure of ideas that forms the basis for a political or economic system.

intuitionism The view that 'good' cannot be further defined but only known through intuition.

justice Used of the ordering of society in a way that reflects established moral principles.

liberalism Used of a political view that emphasizes the freedom of the individual within society.

libertarianism The view that the individual should be free from social and political restraints (as opposed to the more moderate 'Liberal' view that allows freedom only in so far as it does not prevent others from enjoying it also, and thus takes the overall freedom and benefit of society into account).

logos The Greek term for 'word', used by the Stoics for the fundamental rationality in the universe and therefore the basis of a 'natural law' approach to ethics and politics.

metanarrative An overall framework of thought or narrative used to interpret the past (used within the philosophy of history and challenged by post-modernism).

modernism A general term for the self-conscious approach to philosophy and the arts, developed particularly in the first half of the twentieth century.

Natural Law The view that a rational interpretation of the structures of existence can serve as a guide to moral and political thought.

normative Used of an ethical or political argument concerning 'norms' or values (i.e. an argument about what *should* happen, rather than what *does* happen).

normative anthropology A view about the meaning and purpose of human life, expressed in terms of values or 'norms'.

polis Greek term for a city-state (e.g. Ancient Athens).

positive discrimination Refers to the deliberate enhancing of the opportunities available to those groups who might otherwise be deemed to be discriminated against and therefore treated unfairly.

post-modernism A movement in philosophy and the arts which rejects the 'modernist' concept of a self-conscious, authentic, creative self, along with any absolute or global truths, and accepts a relativist view of the variety of cultural and social phenomena.

pragmatism The idea that a theory should be assessed according to its practical use, its implications for other areas of knowledge and its coherence with other beliefs.

preference utilitarianism The utilitarian theory based on the satisfaction of the preferences of the individuals concerned.

prescriptivism The view that, in saying that something is 'right' one is not describing a quality, but 'prescribing' or recommending a course of action.

rationalism The theory that all knowledge is based on reason rather than experience.

relativism The view that there are no absolute truths, but that what is deemed to be true depends on the views of individuals or societies.

scepticism A philosophical view which doubts any claims to knowledge and certainty.

socialism Used of a political view that emphasizes social justice and a concern for the poorer sections of society, and the responsibility of a government to regulate society accordingly.

utilitarianism An ethical theory according to which actions are justified in terms of the anticipated benefit they offer; often summed up as seeking 'the greatest good for the greatest number'.

utopian Used of a description of an ideal state, following the tradition of Thomas Moore's book *Utopia*, describing the political arrangements on a fictional island of that name.

virtue ethics A moral theory based on the development and promotion of qualities and virtues that embody the good life.

taking it further

The following is a short selection of titles that might prove useful for those wanting to further their studies in political philosophy.

Balot, Ryan K. (2006) *Greek Political Thought*, Blackwell.

Blacksell, M. (2006) *Political Geography*, Routledge.

Daniels, N. (1975, 1989) *Reading Rawls*, Stamford University Press.

Fukuyama, F. (2006) *America at the Crossroads: Democracy, Power and the Neoconservative Legacy*, Yale University Press.

Gorz, A. (1994) *Capitalism, Socialism, Ecology*, trans. Chris Turner, Verso.

Hampton, J. (1997) *Political Philosophy*, Westview Press.

Ignatieff, M. (2005) *The Lesser Evil: Political Ethics in an Age of Terror*, Edinburgh Press.

Kymlicka, Will (2002) *Contemporary Political Philosophy* (2nd ed.), OUP.

Miller, D. (2003) *Political Philosophy: a very short introduction*, OUP.

Quill, L. (2006) *Liberty after Liberalism*, Palgrave Macmillan.

Rosen, M. and Wolff, J. (eds) (1999) *Political Thought*, OUP.

Scanlon, T. M. (2003) *The Difficulty of Tolerance*, CUP.

Singer, P. (2004) *The President of Good and Evil: Taking George W. Bush Seriously*, London: Granta Books.

Swift, A. (2006) *Political Philosophy: A Beginners' Guide for Students and Politicians* (second edition), Polity Press.

White, M. J. (2003) *Political Philosophy: An Historical Introduction*, Oxford: Oneworld Publications.

Wolff, J. (2006) *An Introduction to Political Philosophy* (revised edition) Oxford University Press.

In addition to these, the following classic texts are available in various printed editions, and some are available to be downloaded from the web:

Aristotle *Politics*
Augustine *The City of God*
Bentham *Introduction to the Principles of Morals and Legislation*
Berlin *Four Essays on Liberty*
Burke *Reflections on the Revolution in France*
Hobbes *Leviathan*
Locke *Two Treatises on Government*
Machiavelli *The Prince*
Marx *The Communist Manifesto* and *Capital*
Mill *On Liberty* and *The Subjection of Women*
Paine *The Rights of Man*
Plato *The Republic*
Rawls *A Theory of Justice*
Rousseau *The Social Contract*
Wollstonecraft *A Vindication of the Rights of Women*

Philosophy and Ethics

The *Philosophy and Ethics* website, hosted by the author, has a section on political philosophy, providing further suggestions for study, including lists of relevant books and websites on this and related topics.

The author also welcomes comments and questions through that site.

www.philosophyandethics.com

index

teach® yourself

From Advanced Sudoku to Zulu, you'll find everything you need in the **teach yourself** range, in books, on CD and on DVD.

Visit **www.teachyourself.co.uk** for more details.

Advanced Sudoku and Kakuro
Afrikaans
Alexander Technique
Algebra
Ancient Greek
Applied Psychology
Arabic
Arabic Conversation
Aromatherapy
Art History
Astrology
Astronomy
AutoCAD 2004
AutoCAD 2007
Ayurveda
Baby Massage and Yoga
Baby Signing
Baby Sleep
Bach Flower Remedies
Backgammon
Ballroom Dancing
Basic Accounting
Basic Computer Skills
Basic Mathematics
Beauty
Beekeeping
Beginner's Arabic Script
Beginner's Chinese Script
Beginner's Dutch

Beginner's French
Beginner's German
Beginner's Greek
Beginner's Greek Script
Beginner's Hindi
Beginner's Hindi Script
Beginner's Italian
Beginner's Japanese
Beginner's Japanese Script
Beginner's Latin
Beginner's Mandarin Chinese
Beginner's Portuguese
Beginner's Russian
Beginner's Russian Script
Beginner's Spanish
Beginner's Turkish
Beginner's Urdu Script
Bengali
Better Bridge
Better Chess
Better Driving
Better Handwriting
Biblical Hebrew
Biology
Birdwatching
Blogging
Body Language
Book Keeping
Brazilian Portuguese

Bridge
British Citizenship Test, The
British Empire, The
British Monarchy from Henry VIII, The
Buddhism
Bulgarian
Bulgarian Conversation
Business French
Business Plans
Business Spanish
Business Studies
C++
Calculus
Calligraphy
Cantonese
Caravanning
Car Buying and Maintenance
Card Games
Catalan
Chess
Chi Kung
Chinese Medicine
Christianity
Classical Music
Coaching
Cold War, The
Collecting
Computing for the Over 50s
Consulting
Copywriting
Correct English
Counselling
Creative Writing
Cricket
Croatian
Crystal Healing
CVs
Czech
Danish
Decluttering
Desktop Publishing
Detox
Digital Home Movie Making
Digital Photography
Dog Training
Drawing

Dream Interpretation
Dutch
Dutch Conversation
Dutch Dictionary
Dutch Grammar
Eastern Philosophy
Electronics
English as a Foreign Language
English Grammar
English Grammar as a Foreign Language
Entrepreneurship
Estonian
Ethics
Excel 2003
Feng Shui
Film Making
Film Studies
Finance for Non-Financial Managers
Finnish
First World War, The
Fitness
Flash 8
Flash MX
Flexible Working
Flirting
Flower Arranging
Franchising
French
French Conversation
French Dictionary
French for Homebuyers
French Grammar
French Phrasebook
French Starter Kit
French Verbs
French Vocabulary
Freud
Gaelic
Gaelic Conversation
Gaelic Dictionary
Gardening
Genetics
Geology
German
German Conversation

German Grammar
German Phrasebook
German Starter Kit
German Vocabulary
Globalization
Go
Golf
Good Study Skills
Great Sex
Green Parenting
Greek
Greek Conversation
Greek Phrasebook
Growing Your Business
Guitar
Gulf Arabic
Hand Reflexology
Hausa
Herbal Medicine
Hieroglyphics
Hindi
Hindi Conversation
Hinduism
History of Ireland, The
Home PC Maintenance and
  Networking
How to DJ
How to Run a Marathon
How to Win at Casino Games
How to Win at Horse Racing
How to Win at Online Gambling
How to Win at Poker
How to Write a Blockbuster
Human Anatomy & Physiology
Hungarian
Icelandic
Improve Your French
Improve Your German
Improve Your Italian
Improve Your Spanish
Improving Your Employability
Indian Head Massage
Indonesian
Instant French
Instant German
Instant Greek
Instant Italian

Instant Japanese
Instant Portuguese
Instant Russian
Instant Spanish
Internet, The
Irish
Irish Conversation
Irish Grammar
Islam
Israeli-Palestinian Conflict, The
Italian
Italian Conversation
Italian for Homebuyers
Italian Grammar
Italian Phrasebook
Italian Starter Kit
Italian Verbs
Italian Vocabulary
Japanese
Japanese Conversation
Java
JavaScript
Jazz
Jewellery Making
Judaism
Jung
Kama Sutra, The
Keeping Aquarium Fish
Keeping Pigs
Keeping Poultry
Keeping a Rabbit
Knitting
Korean
Latin
Latin American Spanish
Latin Dictionary
Latin Grammar
Letter Writing Skills
Life at 50: For Men
Life at 50: For Women
Life Coaching
Linguistics
LINUX
Lithuanian
Magic
Mahjong
Malay

Managing Stress
Managing Your Own Career
Mandarin Chinese
Mandarin Chinese Conversation
Marketing
Marx
Massage
Mathematics
Meditation
Middle East Since 1945, The
Modern China
Modern Hebrew
Modern Persian
Mosaics
Music Theory
Mussolini's Italy
Nazi Germany
Negotiating
Nepali
New Testament Greek
NLP
Norwegian
Norwegian Conversation
Old English
One-Day French
One-Day French – the DVD
One-Day German
One-Day Greek
One-Day Italian
One-Day Polish
One-Day Portuguese
One-Day Spanish
One-Day Spanish – the DVD
One-Day Turkish
Origami
Owning a Cat
Owning a Horse
Panjabi
PC Networking for Small
  Businesses
Personal Safety and Self
  Defence
Philosophy
Philosophy of Mind
Philosophy of Religion
Phone French
Phone German

Phone Italian
Phone Japanese
Phone Mandarin Chinese
Phone Spanish
Photography
Photoshop
PHP with MySQL
Physics
Piano
Pilates
Planning Your Wedding
Polish
Polish Conversation
Politics
Portuguese
Portuguese Conversation
Portuguese for Homebuyers
Portuguese Grammar
Portuguese Phrasebook
Postmodernism
Pottery
PowerPoint 2003
PR
Project Management
Psychology
Quick Fix French Grammar
Quick Fix German Grammar
Quick Fix Italian Grammar
Quick Fix Spanish Grammar
Quick Fix: Access 2002
Quick Fix: Excel 2000
Quick Fix: Excel 2002
Quick Fix: HTML
Quick Fix: Windows XP
Quick Fix: Word
Quilting
Recruitment
Reflexology
Reiki
Relaxation
Retaining Staff
Romanian
Running Your Own Business
Russian
Russian Conversation
Russian Grammar
Sage Line 50

Sanskrit
Screenwriting
Second World War, The
Serbian
Setting Up a Small Business
Shorthand Pitman 2000
Sikhism
Singing
Slovene
Small Business Accounting
Small Business Health Check
Songwriting
Spanish
Spanish Conversation
Spanish Dictionary
Spanish for Homebuyers
Spanish Grammar
Spanish Phrasebook
Spanish Starter Kit
Spanish Verbs
Spanish Vocabulary
Speaking On Special Occasions
Speed Reading
Stalin's Russia
Stand Up Comedy
Statistics
Stop Smoking
Sudoku
Swahili
Swahili Dictionary
Swedish
Swedish Conversation
Tagalog
Tai Chi
Tantric Sex
Tap Dancing
Teaching English as a Foreign
    Language
Teams & Team Working
Thai
Thai Conversation
Theatre
Time Management
Tracing Your Family History
Training
Travel Writing

Trigonometry
Turkish
Turkish Conversation
Twentieth Century USA
Typing
Ukrainian
Understanding Tax for Small
    Businesses
Understanding Terrorism
Urdu
Vietnamese
Visual Basic
Volcanoes, Earthquakes and
    Tsunamis
Watercolour Painting
Weight Control through Diet &
    Exercise
Welsh
Welsh Conversation
Welsh Dictionary
Welsh Grammar
Wills & Probate
Windows XP
Wine Tasting
Winning at Job Interviews
Word 2003
World Faiths
Writing Crime Fiction
Writing for Children
Writing for Magazines
Writing a Novel
Writing a Play
Writing Poetry
Xhosa
Yiddish
Yoga
Your Wedding
Zen
Zulu

teach yourself

philosophy of religion
mel thompson

- Do you want to investigate religion?
- Would you like to explore what 'God' means?
- Do you want to consider how religion relates to everyday life?

Philosophy of Religion is the essential guide for anyone wanting to understand what religion is about. It explores the key principles upon which religion is based and sets out the arguments for and against belief. Fully updated, this new edition takes into account the different concepts of God and considers religion in light of current concerns such as terrorism, evolution, education and our multi-cultural society.

Mel Thompson is a freelance writer and editor, specializing in philosophy, religion and ethics.

teach
yourself

marx
gill hands

- Do you need an accessible guide to Marx's work?
- Would you like to know more and the man himself?
- Do you want to consider his continuing influence?

Marx is a fascinating guide to the life and works of the 'father of communism'. Get to grips with the key facets of Marx's thought, from his views of philosophy, historical materialism and economic theory to his belief in class struggle and revolution. Consider how his ideas have spread throughout the world, and the influence that they have had in the past and continue to have today.

Gill Hands is an experienced freelance writer of fiction and non-fiction.

philosophy
mel thompson

- Do you need a concise introduction to philosophy?
- Would you like to understand key philosophical arguments?
- Do you want to discover the world's greatest philosophers?

Accessible and jargon-free, **Philosophy** explores the key
philosophical thinkers, arguments and works that have shaped
the society in which we live today. Fully updated and addressing
many contemporary issues, it ensures that complex concepts
are easy to understand. Whether you are a student studying
philosophy at school or university level or just want to discover
this fascinating subject, **Philosophy** is an engaging and
informative read.

Mel Thompson is a freelance writer and editor, specializing in
philosophy, religion and ethics.